ALPHA PROJECT MANAGERS

ALPHA PROJECT MANAGERS
(What the Top 2% Know
That Everyone Else Does Not)

Andy Crowe

Inquiries should be addressed via e-mail to:
info@velociteach.com

First printing, October, 2006

International Standard Book No.
ISBN-13: 978-0-0-9729673-3-8
ISBN-10: 0-9729673-3-8

ATTENTION CORPORATIONS, UNIVERSITIES, COLLEGES, AND PROFESSIONAL ORGANIZATIONS. Quantity discounts are available on bulk purchases of this book. For information, please contact info@velociteach. com.

Table of Contents

Index of Charts and Illustrations

To any project manager who has ever lain awake at night and wondered if there were not a better way.

Introduction

Assumptions can be dangerous things, since people rarely take the time to question or examine them. By definition, we live our lives accepting assumptions. In fact, it is largely impossible to do otherwise.

Most assumptions turn out to be true, but those that do not can be a major setback to individuals, industries, and even entire civilizations. The assumption for centuries that Yellow Fever was caused by "bad air" contributed to the deaths of millions of people. The assumption that a machine that was heavier than air could not fly discouraged people from even trying.

Most of us have a natural resistance to challenging assumptions. When the 19th century Impressionist painters were presented to the established French art schools they were shunned and ridiculed because they did not fall in line with the assumed ideal for art. When Galileo challenged the geocentric model of the universe, he was placed under arrest. Many others throughout history suffered worse fates.

But the payoff to challenging assumptions is that once an assumption is proved to be incorrect, the door to real progress opens. That is why The Alpha

Study, on which this book is based, asked some questions that had already been answered. It tested the assumptions of project managers against those of their stakeholders. In some cases, as you will see, most of us are making incorrect assumptions about what our stakeholders want and how we should relate to them.

The Alpha Study looked at a large group of project managers and stakeholders and challenged many of the assumptions in the profession of project management today; however, it does not represent progress in and of itself. Real progress will begin when the reader approaches the next twelve chapters with an open and introspective mind.

One

The Problem

Us vs. Them

It has been said that solutions hold no intrinsic value. A solution by itself is worthless unless there is a problem that needs solving. Today, the project management world is awash in solutions ranging from software to maturity models, to methodologies, to training courses. This would be fine if we all agreed upon and understood the problem.

Project management has become the *sine qua non* of the business world. Years ago, if you were a white-collar professional, you needed computer skills to succeed, and seemingly overnight, those who could use a computer proficiently were segregated from those who could not. Today, however, basic computer skills are ubiquitous within the work place, and among managers and aspiring leaders the indispensable skill is rapidly becoming project management. Businesses rise and fall as a result of projects. They are the engines of any organization. Without solid project management, the best strategies never materialize into tangible results. Vision may abound, but without the ability to carry it out, the results are lacking. Now, the indispensable skill for the white collar world has become basic project management. Projects generate results, and project managers who can deliver these results typically rise quickly through their organization.

The project managers who are truly able to deliver real value, however, are few and far between, and project managers who can consistently manage a project and the process of delivery are scarce indeed. In fact, the problem is worse than we realize. When Price Waterhouse Coopers conducted a 21st century survey of 200 global companies about their project management maturity, they found that over half of all projects fail, and only a meager 2.5% of corporations consistently meet their targets for scope, time, and cost.

This has led corporations to initiate projects with no real expectations that the goals and constraints will be met. Project managers routinely shift the blame for failure to customers for not understanding the process. Teams regularly mutiny when the burden is shifted to them, and senior management grows ever more frustrated that most project managers do not seem to understand the basics of solution delivery and fundamental management principles.

Project managers know there is a problem, but we do not agree on its definition. We are spending untold millions on software and process improvements to address the problem, and yet until we clearly identify the problem, it will defy our best attempts to solve it.

While there are various culprits and systemic reasons behind this problem, one stands out in particular. As Walt Kelly famously quipped, "*We have met the enemy, and he is us.*"

We are the problem. Project managers. Not bosses. Not unmotivated teams. And especially not customers. "He is us."

Most project managers do not want to hear this. It is easier to complain about our team, to grouse about our flawed organizational structures, and to roll our eyes at the customer's ignorance or naivety. It is much easier to blame misfortune on others than it is to be introspective.

It is also less effective. Customers are largely out of our control. Project managers can influence the customer's thoughts and decisions, but we cannot control them. The same goes for senior management, and even the team. This leads us to a bit of good news, however. The good news is that while most of the other factors we traditionally blame are well outside of our sphere of control, we do have ultimate control over ourselves. The good news is that if we are essentially the problem, then we can also be the solution.

Practice Makes... Something

One of the early lessons for many children is that practice makes perfect. While the lesson is intended to bring home the importance of discipline and the pursuit of improvement, its message is fundamentally flawed.

Practice does not make perfect. Endless repetitions of a golf swing with an incorrect stance will never lead to the long distance drive, the consistency, or the accuracy you want. Practicing bad handwriting will not eventually produce a beautiful script. Practicing the trumpet with a flawed embouchure will not produce the pure tone or precision the musician craves.

Indeed, practice does not make perfect, nor has it ever. Wrong practice only reinforces wrong behavior. For the athlete, muscle memory develops with repetition, and even a tiny flaw may take years to unlearn and correct. For the professional project manager, when mistakes are put into practice, not only do bad results follow, but bad patterns emerge. Over time, it becomes harder to escape these patterns, and they begin to form entire industry trends. Over time, we are led to the place where project managment is in the spotlight, and yet, over 50% of our projects fail.

How many project managers secretly know that they are repeating the same mistakes time and again? They fall into problematic patterns in the way they motivate their team, or in the way they relate to the customer, or perhaps it is the way they fail to manage the scope or to track actuals against the plan. They frustrate their organizations through repeated patterns of poor communication, and ultimately these become things we simply grow to accept.

When unacceptable project results arise, project managers have often resorted to blame. It may be that we blame the team, insufficient support, the process, the lack of process, bad luck, or most often the customer. The more likely reality is that we never really learned to practice the art of project management.

When a project is managed well, it is a thing of beauty. Team effort is channeled and orchestrated like a symphony. Urgency is focused in the right areas and at the right times. Order emerges instead of chaos. Status reports read like an interesting story. Communication flows freely, and it makes sense. The team is in support of the project, and the project is in support of the organization's goals. The customer, the team, and the organization all support and trust the project manager, and for good reason. This is the way it should be.

As a profession, one of the main misconceptions we have bought into is that the more you know, the better the project manager you will be. Knowledge of project management is a necessity; however, by itself it is wholly insufficient. As Mark Twain said, "*It ain't what you don't know that gets you into trouble. It's what you know for sure that just ain't so.*" If one practices a flawed golf swing for many years, he may even go so far as to instruct others in that technique, further propagating the problem, while firmly believing that he is helping the other person.

Experience is another test we've put into place, assuming that the more experience the project manager has, the better. As discussed earlier, this is true only if it was the right kind of experience. Bad practice does not lead to good results, and bad experience does not eventually make a good project manager. Learning from mistakes is of tremendous value, but learning from doing it right is a necessary component as well. It is not valuable experience if a project manager has only done things the wrong way for ten years.

One of the great shortcomings the profession of project management faces today is that very few project managers have ever been taught how to manage a project. We have been taught about project management. We have read books, taken classes, and even managed projects. We have learned process and theory, but the majority of us have never been taught how to actually manage a project from conception through closure. It is no wonder that projects and our stakeholders are suffering the way they are. And it is not just projects that are suffering. Organizations are suffering, teams are suffering, and perhaps the project managers are suffering most of all. The comparison can be made to a medical student having taken all of the right classes but never having worked alongside an experienced medical doctor. This person stands to do more harm than good.

And so, accepting that practice alone will likely make things worse, but that perfect practice makes perfect, we are led to the obvious question: Where do we learn to practice project management perfectly?

In any discipline, the way to improve is to study the experts in that field. Mastery occurs not so much in learning the basics, but in the perfection of nuance. In general, project managers do not lack for studying the basics of project management. The theoretical framework and knowledge are largely in place, but the ability to execute flawlessly is as rare as ever. This leaves us in a situation not too different from that of a person who has studied fly fishing his whole life but who has never learned to perfect his cast with a smooth arc. The knowledge is there, at least in part, but the perfect practice is not.

The Alpha Study, on which this book is based, set out to find project managers who are at the top of their "game." It is built upon the simple premise that we have something to learn from the top practitioners in our profession. More than simply possessing knowledge, they are producing consistent results, effectively managing teams, and delivering value to customers and senior management. In order to qualify as an Alpha, there were very few other requirements. Educational degrees and certification were not prerequisites, although most of those who qualified as Alphas in this study were both well-educated and certified project managers.

By studying the people who operate above the everyday problems that plague our profession, we can move past the basics and work on perfecting the nuances of our craft. This book takes the perspective that project management is a pursuit that is not learned quickly but is perfected over a career.

We are the problem, but as this book explores, we are also the solution.

Two α

The Alpha Study

The Alpha Study initially began by inviting 3,000 project managers to participate and was narrowed down to 860 who were able to participate fully.

The results of the Alpha Study challenge several long-held beliefs about successful project managers, including how they prioritize their time and how they relate to various stakeholders.

This chapter briefly explains how the Alpha Study was conducted and answers some of the questions that will likely be raised as the reader approaches this book.

First of all, it is important to understand what the Alpha Study is not. Although it was conducted carefully, it is not a scientific study. The group of participants was not purely randomly selected. Instead, they came from the customer list of Velociteach, a project management education company. While this does not invalidate the participants in any way, it could have an influence on some outcomes. For instance, all participants were people who had received some kind of project management training in the previous five years. Any underlying factor, however subtle, may influence the outcome of such a study, and the Alpha Study attempted to overcome this by using a larger sample size in order to draw more accurate conclusions about the overall population. The real value of the study was in the aggregated trends, which are explored throughout this book.

The Alpha Study was conducted over a nine-month period, with 860 project manager participants. In order to participate in the study, the project managers had to have met several criteria:

- They had to be currently practicing project management, and they had to have been practicing project management for a minimum of 7,500 hours over the previous five year period. As most of them had recently received training for project management certification, this requirement was met by the majority.

- They had to have worked for the same organization for the previous three years, although both contract and permanent employment were acceptable.

- Project managers were required to have their bosses participate, which cut the field down significantly.

- Participants had to find three team members who had reported to the project manager over the past calendar year for at least 500 hours each.

- The project managers had to have a customer who would participate in the study. The customer could be any customer who had received product, services, or results from the project manager over the previous three-year period.

- The project managers and their stakeholders who participated in the Alpha Study had to respond to a two-part survey rolled out over a period of twelve weeks. After that, specific participants were chosen for personal follow-up interviews on specific topics.

- Finally, the project managers had to have managed at least one project with a total budget of at least $75,000 over the previous twelve months.

- None of the participants would receive compensation for their participation.

The initial group was pared down to include 860 project managers, who provided 4,398 stakeholders in various roles for a total pool of 5,258 project managers and stakeholders.

In order to help people feel comfortable with the process, it was made clear to everyone who participated in the Alpha Study that their responses would be kept in the strictest confidence and would not be shared with anyone outside the study. In other words, bosses' comments were not going to be shared with the project manager, nor were customer's thoughts to be communicated back to the team. Survey participants could speak freely about their projects, their challenges, and their careers.

The surveys were conducted using a combination of web-based surveys and interviews, and the results were imported into spreadsheets and analytical software to perform numerical analysis.

The focus of the book is on the top 2% of the whole survey population. Eighteen people (roughly 2%) were selected as the Alphas out of the entire 860 project managers who participated. Their qualification as Alphas was based solely on meeting the minimum criteria and the responses of the stakeholders.

In part one of the survey, stakeholders were asked to confidentially rank the project manager's performance. Each stakeholder was asked to rank their project manager on a scale from 1 to 100 on the following ten dimensions:

1. Rate the project manager's overall performance
    at setting your expectations and the
    expectations of other project stakeholders.

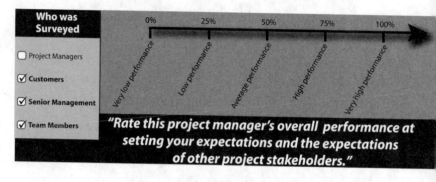

"Rate this project manager's overall performance at setting your expectations and the expectations of other project stakeholders."

2. Rate the project manager's overall performance
    at communicating efficiently and effectively to
    you and others throughout the project.

3. Rate the project manager's overall performance
    at managing your issues and the issues of
    others.

4. Rate the project manager's overall performance
    at identifying and managing risk to the
    appropriate level for the project.

5. Rate the project manager's overall performance
    at leadership of the project team.

6. Rate the project manager's overall performance at meeting the scope, quality, time, and budget baselines for the project.

7. Rate the project manager's overall performance at managing the procurement process and vendors, where applicable.

8. Rate the project manager's overall performance at managing change to the project.

9. Rate the project manager's overall performance at balancing competing stakeholder objectives to deliver an optimal solution.

10. Rate the project manager's overall performance at delivering a product, service, or result that met your expectations.

Once the responses were tallied, the stakeholders of the project managers who qualified as the top 2% were contacted for further discussion and to make sure they responded accurately, and these follow-up interviews did impact the results.

Each of the ten items listed previously was weighted the same; however, the stakeholders did not all have equal voices. For the purposes of this study, the stakeholders' votes were allocated as follows:

• Senior Management: 30%
• Team Members: 30%
• Customer: 40%

Stakeholder Voice in the Alpha Study

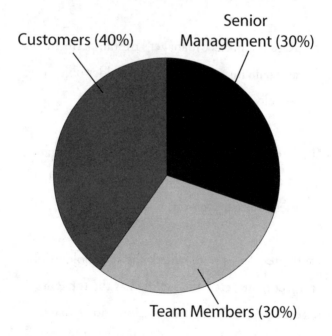

This gave the customer the most important voice in the process, but not so much that it drowned out the team or the organization.

While are were many other factors discussed throughout this book, the previous ten aspects made up the backbone of the Alpha ranking. The composite scores were tallied, and the top 2% were selected, and although many items of interest were measured in the Alpha Study, many more were not. The reader will not find any statistics about race, geographical trends, religious affiliation, or political leaning. One of the more glaring omissions from this study was the effect of project management certification on a project manager's ranking. The reason for this is simple. Nearly 100% of the 860 project managers came from a list of people who had received project management certification training. All of the Alphas had at least one project management certification, but that fact is misleading, since almost all of the other 842 non-Alphas did as well.

The questions for the project managers were entirely different than those asked of the stakeholders. For the most part, the study was not interested in whether a project manager believed that he or she was an Alpha. Instead, it focused on their practices. Part one of the study focused on the performance aspects and asked "what" the Alphas were doing differently than everyone else. Part two of the survey delved deeper into belief, experience, and attitude and asked "why." Finally, post-survey interviews were conducted with each of the Alphas and their stakeholders, as well as a representative sample from the non-Alpha group. These surveys ensured that the data gathered from the surveys told the right story about who they were and how they thought about and executed their work.

While the study technically included participants from the continents of North America, South America, Africa, Asia, and Europe, the population was very heavily concentrated in North America. This concentration had an unavoidable impact on the results. Although the factors that contribute to a project manager's success are largely common no matter where they live, regional and cultural variances will color the outcomes. For instance, there were no controls in place to determine whether a score of 90 out of 100 in Africa is equivalent to a 90 out of 100 in Asia. Also, in some parts of Europe, one is considered the highest, and 100 the lowest. This could serve to confuse some participants and unintentionally color the results. Therefore, the survey should be taken for what it is: a study of the factors that influence a project manager's success that comes from a highly North American-centric view.

One noticeable result of the data is that the results were normally distributed, which made the overall analysis more straightforward.

The top 2% of project managers were selected simply because they exemplified a significant gap from the other 98%, and it is that gap, both in performance and knowledge, that is the subject of this book. Although it may be tempting to focus on the individuals, the focus should actually be on the trends revealed by the data.

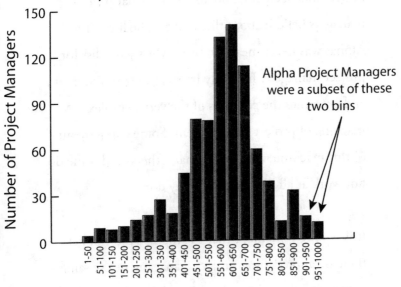

Alpha Project Managers were a subset of these two bins

The Greek stoic, Heraclites, said that you cannot step into the same river twice. Life is ever-changing and fluid. This study produced a unique list of 18 individuals. It provides a snapshot of a point in time, but this book is not about a list of people or their organizations or industries. It is about what a group of high-performers were doing differently than the other project managers at that point in time. This group is also fluid and dynamic, and it is entirely probable that the same study, repeated a year later, would produce a very different list.

This book challenges some long-held beliefs about project management, and also about what project managers believe about themselves. The list of the Alphas was never meant to be a "who's who" list for project managers. It simply freezes time for a moment and examines the contents of the very complex machine of project management. Some components of this machine work better than others, and some do not work at all like we think they do.

It is wise to remember that the top 2% did not get there by approaching project management the same way as everyone else or by doing their jobs exactly the same way. Subsequent chapters in this book provide the reader with the opportunity to look at the art and science of project management from different perspectives.

Three

Meet the Alphas

In any field, there are individuals who excel. This book focuses on the individuals who excel at project management. The Alpha group consists of six females and twelve males, which was a reasonably close approximation of the ratio of the overall population of 860 managers who participated in the study.

These are 18 individuals who are doing things right. They are consistently delivering projects that meet the project goals, managing stakeholder expectations, and keeping the customer, the team, and the organization in harmony. In other words, they are doing what many project managers find to be impossible.

While most of this book is about what the 18 Alphas are doing differently than the 842 others, this chapter presents a brief biographical sketch of each of the Alphas and their background. Additionally, each of them was asked to write a short paragraph about project management and what they have learned in their careers.

In order to encourage people to speak freely throughout this study, names were changed in order to protect identities. All other information provided is accurate.

Name: Angela
Age: 44
Industry: Travel

Angela lives in the Northeastern United States and works for a company in the travel industry, providing online technology and solutions to corporate customers. Her job requires frequent travel, putting her in front of customers on a weekly basis. On average, Angela manages two projects at a time, occasionally spiking up to three. When she joined the organization ten years ago, project management was basically unknown to them. Angela is married with three children and holds both a Bachelors and a Masters degree in Finance.

"My boss was hired in to create the PMO about five years ago, and that has had a tremendous impact on my work. He made sure we had a process in place and he made sure we all were trained on how it should work, and things really did start to run a lot smoother at that point. Before then, the project managers (myself included) were ready to jump out the window. Nothing was being captured, and no one was improving. Over the past five years, a lot of faith in project management has been restored, with us and our customers."

Name: Brandon
Age: 51
Industry: Aviation

Brandon lives in the Northern United States and works for an aircraft manufacturer. His position is responsible for the development of new aircraft products and the modification of existing components. The job requires deep expertise and the ability to communicate technical information with the engineering department as well as to communicate the business aspects of the project to C-Suite management. Brandon is married with two grown children. He holds a Masters degree in Aerospace Engineering.

"I started my career as an engineer, and for years, I wanted nothing to do with management. After working for almost a decade in project management, I think I've learned that projects get done through process and people, and you can't ignore one side or the other. As an engineer, it would be easy for me to elevate the process over the people, but it really has to be the other way around if you are going to make a career in project management."

Name: Brenda
Age: 34
Industry: Beverage

Brenda works for a soft drink and beverage company on the East Coast of the United States. Her projects center around collateral products and market studies that take place when a new beverage is introduced.

Her typical project budgets range from $250,000 to $2,000,000, and because of the impact these projects can have on the company's bottom line, accurate measurement and reporting is critical to her job. Brenda is a divorced mother of two. She holds a Bachelors and a Masters degree in Marketing.

"I believe the best project management takes place before the project begins. A good PM will begin managing expectations from the first mention of an assignment. I learned this the hard way after a couple of successive projects were assigned to me with the budget, time, and scope already set in stone, and of course, they were completely unrealistic. I thought that I was supposed to put on a good face and do my best, but that turned out to be bad for everyone involved. The best thing I can do for the customer, the team, and my boss is to set their expectations realistically. That can ruffle some fur at the beginning, but it keeps me from giving my profession a bad name."

Name: Calvin

Age: 58

Industry: Financial Services

Calvin has worked for the same financial services organization in the Northeastern United States for 23 years, and that career has put him in eight different departments with ten different bosses. He has worked as project manager now for the last seven years. His projects are typically kiosk-based applications and are targeted toward retail customers. Calvin is single and holds a Bachelors degree in Finance and a Masters degree in Business Administration.

"My whole life changed when I finally understood that there was a process for doing this job. At first, it changed for the worse, because I didn't understand the process, but after a while I started learning how these different pieces fit together, and it all started to fit into place. The first part of my discovery was figuring out what to do, and the second part of it was figuring out how to do it. Now I wouldn't change out of project management for anything."

Name: Cheryl

Age: 44

Industry: Automotive

Cheryl works with a company in the Western United States that designs and manufactures electrical components and sound systems that are factory-installed in new automobiles. This position requires significant collaboration with outside partners and negotiating skills to ensure that both her customer and her organization are well-represented in the process. She holds a Bachelors degree in Electrical Engineering and a Masters degree in Management.

"My current job requires me to work with so many people from so many different disciplines, and I am the one who has to bring them all together into a product. For me, accurately defining the scope is the most difficult part. I've seen small assumptions that weren't documented end up costing hundreds of thousands of dollars when manufacturing kicked in. If I get the scope right, then most times, the rest of the project falls into place."

Name: Dan

Age: 33

Industry: Information Technology

Dan is a Canadian and is tied for the youngest Alpha project manager. He works for a global consulting organization, managing their technology infrastructure and large-scale enterprise deployments of hardware and software to as many as 10,000 desktops at a time. He holds an undergraduate degree in Computer Science and is married with one child.

"For me, most of project management means planning, and most of my planning really translates into risk evaluation. I have to make sure that we consider every possible ramification of actions we take. The worst case is that my team could cripple the whole enterprise, bringing all the desktops or servers down, so I plan, evaluate, plan some more. Then I make sure we execute exactly according to the plan. At the end, we archive our plans and discuss what we should have done differently. I've been doing this for four years now, so the plans we have are getting pretty mature, but the technology is constantly changing, and we have quite a few remote users, so that keeps things interesting."

Name: Dave
Age: 56
Industry: Insurance

Dave is a project manager based in the Midwestern
United States, and he has worked with three different
insurance companies over his 36-year career. He has
been with his current organization for fourteen years
and has worked as project manager for the last nine
years. He holds a Bachelors degree in Political Science.

*"Insurance is all about risk, but the insurance industry is
famous for having a very low tolerance for risk. I started
my career in insurance being low risk as well, but I've
since found that there is simply no substitute for failure.
I have learned much more from the project failures I've
been involved with than I have from the successes, and
I believe organizations are the same way. Organizations
make mistakes just like people do, and they learn just like
people do. Failure can be better than any training class as
long as you have the right culture and as long as there is a
process in place for capturing the lessons learned."*

Name: Jarred

Age: 40

Industry: Transportation and Logistics

Jarred works for a logistics company located on the West Coast of the United States. His projects focus on the development and deployment of hardware and software-based RFID solutions to help companies manage and track inventory in real time. His projects typically develop smaller add-on solutions to present to market. He has been with the same organization for sixteen years, and he has been a project manager there for the last seven years. Jarred is married and holds undergraduate degrees in Transportation Engineering and Management.

"I believe a project manager is only as good as his team. I put a lot of time into selecting my team for a project, and I make sure they are the right ones for the job. I try to avoid turnover and try to keep working on team-strengthening throughout the project. If you get the right team members in place, over time, the project will run itself. With the wrong people in place, you can work as hard as you like, and you'll miss your targets. I just wish I had figured this out years ago!"

Name: Jeff
Age: 38
Industry: Software Development

Jeff works for a commercial software company as a senior project manager in the Northwestern United States. He oversees projects related to a suite of products that make up nearly 40% of his organization's annual revenue. Because of the critical nature of his role, he has "dotted line" reporting relationships to eight separate senior managers. He holds a Bachelors degree in Computer Science and a Masters degree in Project Management.

"Like a lot of people in Information Technology, I've struggled with how to implement process. Last year I led our efforts to become CMM Level 4, and that project was actually one of the most difficult I've ever tackled. The one thing I have done that has helped me more than anything else is to have a mentor. My mentor is the CIO of another company, and he has helped me to sift through the issues in my job and to focus on what is important. I started out as a coder, and I can say, without reservation, that project management is much more challenging. With software, once you get it developed, you expect it to run trouble-free, but with projects, you're always wondering what potential disaster is waiting around the next corner."

Name: Jim
Age: 48
Industry: Construction

Jim is a senior program manager for an engineering firm in the Mid-Atlantic United States where he has worked for eight years. He performs projects specializing in demolition, site preparation, and new construction, and for the past three years, he has performed projects almost exclusively in South America. Despite his title, Jim's role is that of project manager, with primary responsibility for overseeing the planning, execution, and control of individual projects. Jim has a Bachelors degree in Civil Engineering and is married with one child.

"In my business, we always run the potential of getting caught between the customer and the team. Everybody is angling on the project for what they can squeeze out of it, and so I'm constantly representing the customer's interests to the team, and the team's interests to the customer. I believe that on larger projects, half of my job is arbitration. I'm constantly trying to put this whole thing together in such a way that it all works."

Name: Kyle

Age: 41

Industry: Information Technology Outsourcing

Kyle has worked for the same organization for sixteen years, and he transitioned into the outsourcing division eight years ago. His job has moved him around the United States and currently has him based in the Midwest. His job responsibilities span both project management and account management. Kyle holds a Masters degree in Business Administration and a Project Management Masters certificate. Kyle is married with four children.

"My job requires me to be super detail-focused. If one small thing gets overlooked, then it could cost my company a lot of money, as well as a lot of jobs. We have a pretty involved process in place for making sure nothing gets missed, but the real trick for me is to make sure we have a well-rounded team in place. I am not the most detail-oriented person in the world, so I make sure I have those people on the team. One person can't possibly do it all, but the right team can."

Name: Lori

Age: 33

Industry: Strategic Outsourcing

Tied for the position of the youngest Alpha, Lori works for a strategic outsourcing company on the West Coast of the United States. Her job is focused on helping mid-size and large organizations outsource business processes, specifically in the service sector. She is typically assigned projects that are in the pre-sales cycle, and she carries them through until they are ready to be fully handed off to operations. She is single and holds a Bachelors degree in Philosophy.

"I view my projects more like living organisms than linear processes. It is people who handle the details and people who get the work done, and people who talk to the customer. It's my job to keep the organism healthy. I really believe that rather than looking at a project as a set of processes, we should treat it as a system. It's just much easier to make everything work that way."

Name: Marty

Age: 62

Industry: Defense Industry

Marty works in the defense industry in the Middle Atlantic United States after a lengthy career in the United States Army. He manages classified projects with the Department of Homeland Security with teams of fifteen to twenty direct reports and numerous suppliers. Marty holds an undergraduate degree in Criminology and is divorced with one adult child.

"One of the things I have often seen on corporate projects where we interface is a void of leadership. This is one of the biggest opportunities out there. I come from a military background, and there, it is all about leadership. I believe that a lot of projects in the corporate world are being run by people who are probably pretty smart, but they don't have a grasp of what it really means to lead."

Name: Melinda
Age: 39
Industry: Biotechnology

Melinda works in a biotechnical firm in the Northeastern United States, working on projects to create new consumer products. Her projects typically go through numerous approval processes, ranging from internal approval, to approval with various governments, to market-based customer-acceptance studies. Melinda has worked in this role for six years. She holds a Ph.D. in Biotechnology and is married with two children.

"When I first got out of school, I worked a ridiculous number of hours each week. When I became the project manager, it got even worse. It took me a long time, and one failed marriage, to learn to take care of myself. In my industry, project management will kill you if you let it, because people are always rushing products to market and trying to get things out the door in crazy timeframes. I make sure that I am in good mental and physical health each day, and I do the same thing for my team. I think the company appreciates this, because we have very low turnover in my group, and people are generally happy, and it shows in the quality of work they do."

Name: Sarah
Age: 37
Industry: Telecommunications

Sarah works for a telecommunications company
headquartered in the Western United States, where
she has worked since earning her graduate degree
in management at the age of 25. She is one of over
twenty project managers in her organization who
work to roll out new products to mobile users.
Sarah is married with one child, and she holds
dual Bachelors degrees in Marketing and Business
Administration, as well as a Masters degree in Business
Administration.

*"To me, the size of the project is rarely the issue. It might
be the issue if you were doing it all yourself, but it really
isn't the point if you have a team in place. The real point
is whether you are going to do things the right way and
follow a process. We have this really great methodology
that, if you buy into it, helps projects run so much more
smoothly, and it becomes a contest to see who can follow
the process the best. Whether the project is large or small
becomes less relevant."*

Name: Sudhir

Age: 44

Industry: Retail

Sudhir works for a mid-sized retailer in the Southern United States, managing supplier-based projects to increase their logistical efficiency and sales. According to his senior manager, his projects had a direct return on investment of over 4,000% in the previous fiscal year alone. Sudhir is married with one child, and he holds a Masters degree in Computer Science.

"The best project managers that I have worked with just seem to make things easy. It's hard to describe, but the way a project runs is so much smoother with these project managers. There isn't as much fighting or arguing over things that don't advance the project, and I have tried to mirror my practices on this as well. It isn't that we won't ever have arguments or conflict, but I make sure it is constructive as much as it lies within my power."

Name: Thomas

Age: 49

Industry: Commercial Software

Thomas works for a commercial software company in the Southern United States, where he has been for twelve years. His projects focus on feature releases of software that often span several years between major deliverables. He holds a Bachelors degree in Chemistry and a Bachelors and a Masters degree in Project Management. He is married with one adult child.

"I have come to think about major projects as being like political campaigns. You have to respond in real-time to emerging threats. You have to call in favors. You have to scramble to explain news, whether it is good or bad. On top of that, the best plans in the world can be turned upside down in an instant. My two big takeaways over the past decade have been to keep relationships with others, and I don't just mean the team, in good shape, and to be flexible. These have come into play on every successful major project I've worked on."

Name: Victor

Age: 38

Industry: Business Process Consulting

Victor is a project manager who focuses on business management and operational efficiency consulting in the Southwest United States. His projects are often bid on a percent of savings to the customer, making up-front planning and efficient execution critical. Victor has worked with his current organization for three years, and prior to that, he worked for a competing company. He holds a Masters degree in Information Technology, and a Masters certificate in Project Management, and is married with two children.

"Toward the end of some projects I've worked on, the managers made their teams work these really long hours. After the second or third time this happened, I just assumed that this was the way things went. Then I got to work with a manager who planned everything out really well and ran the team at a good pace the whole time, and we kept on schedule. When the customer found out that things were on schedule, he kept trying to increase the scope, but we had a good manager this time,

and she wouldn't let him do it without adjusting the baselines. That was the first time I was on a project that finished everything on time and on budget, and I was amazed at how easy she made it look. It took me more than one project to strike the right balance there, but I finally started finishing most projects on time and within budget. Contrary to popular belief, it is achievable, but the project manager really has to manage in order to make it work."

The Top 2%

These 18 individuals represent the top 2% of all project managers in The Alpha Study. They are the primary focus of this book. Each chapter studies what they did differently than the other 842 who participated in the study, and after understanding what was different, the study probed why it was different.

Sometimes, the differences in attitude or approach are dramatic, but most often they are subtle. Regardless of what else we may think, it is important to rememeber that their approach works in the eyes of stakeholders.

In the next chapter, we will explore how the attitude of these 18 differs from the rest of the group and how that influences project success. Subsequent chapters will explore the effect of other attributes. Now that we have met the Alphas, let's explore what the top 2% know that everyone else does not.

Four α

Attitude and Belief

Over the past half-century, there has been a strong body of research that supports the theory that attitude can have a profound impact on a manager's ability to lead, and it has been strongly linked to job promotions and salary. But how does it affect the project manager's ability to satisfy stakeholders? Can attitude have an impact on the work the project manager does? Can a project manager's attitude influence his or her ability, real or perceived, to deliver results on a project?

During in-depth interviews with the Alpha group and representative samples from the non-Alphas, several distinct characteristics emerged in the area of the project manager's attitude toward work. Alphas looked forward to work more often, and although they maintained similar stress levels while on the job, they were significantly less anxious about work when they were not on the job. Their senior managers, customers, and teams ranked them as having a more positive disposition, and as a group, the Alphas also indicated much lower levels of "Sunday Afternoon Depression" when facing another workweek.

Succinctly put, Alphas enjoy work more than their counterparts.

It does not take a vivid imagination to conjure up several possible explanations for these findings. Perhaps Alphas work on more enjoyable projects, and thus enjoy their jobs more. Also, the Alphas earn 21% more in gross annual income than the average non-Alpha, which could contribute to their overall job satisfaction. Or perhaps Alphas simply work in better project environments with more agreeable managers or better organizations.

While all of these reasons could be contributing factors, post-survey interviews revealed other significant drivers. Before exploring the underlying reasons, however, let's take a look at the survey results for job satisfaction.

Survey participants were asked to rank the degree to which they agreed with the following statement: "On the whole, I generally love my job."

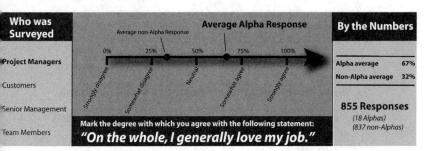

All participants were asked to quantify their response on a scale from 1 to 100. This particular statement was left intentionally vague, not allowing participants to qualify or explain their answers in this round of the survey. On average, Alphas' support of that statement was over double that of the non-Alpha group.

Although this question only captures an attitude at a single point in time, much like a snapshot, it delivered one of the most dramatic differences in responses between the Alphas and non-Alphas. By and large, Alphas are more content with their jobs, but this begs the question, "Do Alphas love their work because they are Alphas, or are they Alphas, in part, because they love their jobs?" To try and understand this difference, survey participants were interviewed in more detail.

Cheryl, an Alpha in the automotive industry, said, "*I found early in my career that loving my job is a decision I have to make every day. It doesn't come naturally for me, but if I decide that I'm going to love my work, it makes a difference in how I work and in how I choose to see things. Over time, I really have grown to love my job, but that started out as a choice. It certainly didn't happen automatically.*"

Another difference that emerged in the subsequent interviews was that Alphas tend to treat project management like a career, while non-Alphas are more likely to view project management as a stepping stone. This sometimes subtle difference in attitude has far-reaching implications in how the project manager views his or her job and how the project manager is viewed by the organization and stakeholders. For instance, if one project manager believes that she is in this position for the long haul, she is likely to perform differently than a project manager who believes that she may only be doing this job for a relatively short time. The project manager who believes that she will be in this position long term is likely to nurture relationships with team members and co-managers, while the one with a "short-timer" mentality may be tempted to sacrifice relationships for results. The former attitude, as we will see in Chapter Eight, fosters an investment that pays dividends for the project manager throughout her career, while the latter may well work against the project manager on current and future projects.

Project Management As A Career Path

Since Alphas view their job as a career more often than non-Alphas, they are also more likely to seek out training and education that directly applies to their work. Survey participants were asked to indicate the number of hours of job-related training they had completed over the past three years (not restricted to project management training). Alphas responded that they had participated in an average of 19% more training than their counterparts.

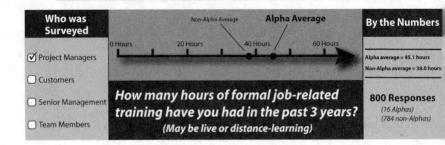

The data did show a surprisingly high number of hours of training received by the 800 responses to this question; however, it should be pointed out that the survey list was derived from a list of project managers who had received project management training in the past five years, which may explain, in part, the unexpected rightward shift in the following graph.

Distribution of All Responses
(Includes Alpha and non-Alpha)

Whether Alphas seek out more training or more training contributes to the project manager becoming an Alpha presents a chicken-egg type question. In reality, it is likely that the two factors contribute to each other, but the fact that Alphas engage in more training deserves attention.

But what about the environment in which they work? Do Alphas work for better organizations than their counterparts? Or do they receive better projects or work for better bosses or customers?

Interestingly, the data here pointed to a resounding "maybe." Due to the nature of the study, a project manager could not qualify as an "Alpha" unless he or she received top marks from senior management, and in structuring the study this way, it was highly likely that senior managers of Alphas would be generally favorable toward project management. Of course, the argument could be made that these senior managers were more favorable toward project management because of the way the Alphas were doing their job.

After analyzing organizations where project management is a respected discipline and contrasting with organizations where project management is looked at as a necessary evil (at best), it is little surprise that the project managers working in environments where their profession is valued are more likely to be successful. Again, the two factors likely contribute to each other. Alphas almost certainly raise awareness and value of project management within an organization. At the same time, being in an organization that values project management is practically a prerequisite to being an Alpha.

The Perception of Authority

Another element of attitude that was probed was the level of authority that project managers have on their projects. Do Alphas have more authority than their counterparts within the organization to make the critical decisions and manage the project?

They certainly believe they do.

When asked to quantify the degree to which they agreed with the statement, "I have adequate authority to manage the projects for which I am responsible," the average response of the Alpha group was between

"Agree" and "Strongly Agree," while the remaining 98% of those surveyed had a more pessimistic perception of their authority. Their average response landed between Neutral and Somewhat Disagree. In other words, the non-Alpha project managers felt that they did not have adequate authority to match their responsibility. Perhaps the most surprising element of this was that 20% of the non-Alpha project managers strongly disagreed with the statement.

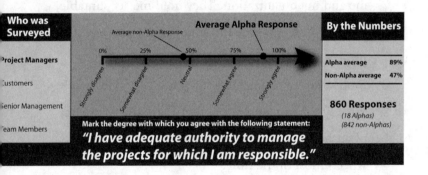

Victor, an Alpha project manager at a consulting firm, explained his response this way. "*When I am assigned to manage a project, I have to assume I have the authority I need unless specifically stated otherwise. It would be a complete waste of time for me to spend my time wondering if I have adequate authority. You have to take the bull by the horns and get started. I honestly don't think I'd accept a project where I knew going into it that I didn't have the authority I needed to deliver it successfully.*"

Another Alpha, Melinda, said, "*My reputation rides on every project I manage. Authority is basically a proxy for trust, and if my boss trusts me, then the authority is easy to come by. I have to have the authority if I'm the manager. I've also found that it's best to live by the motto that it's easier to ask forgiveness than permission.*"

Contrast this with Jerry, a non-Alpha at a Fortune 50 company. "This hits on the big struggle between me and my organization. They hold me accountable, but they don't give me the authority to manage the project. At my company, people have very little motivation to cooperate with you if they don't work directly for you, and if you don't have the right level of authority on the project, you end up spinning your wheels most of the time."

But what happens when senior management is asked to define the degree to which their project managers have the necessary authority to manage the project? Senior managers of surveyed project managers were asked to respond to the following statement: "This project manager has the necessary organizational authority to manage the project successfully."

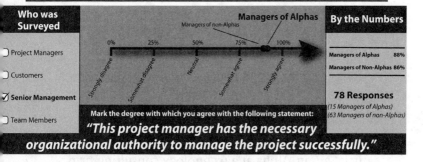

There was virtually no difference between the responses! In other words, senior managers of both Alphas and non-Alphas believed that they had empowered their project managers with the appropriate level of authority to manage the project.

It should also be noted that the Alphas and their senior managers were in total agreement about their level of authority, with the Alpha response averaging 89%, and senior management's response averaging 88%. The great disconnect is between the non-Alphas and their managers. In this case, there was a 39% gap between their responses, with the non-Alphas reporting a gloomy average of 47%, while their managers pegged their authority at 86% on a scale from 1 to 100. From senior management's point of view, Alphas and non-Alphas had virtually the same level of organizational authority.

This perception of authority, whether high or low, reaches far into the project, affecting the way the Alphas or non-Alphas manage conflict, assign team members, and resolve issues.

Alicia, a non-Alpha at a technology consulting firm, inadvertently addressed the heart of the issue when she said, "*I feel like my team would take me more seriously if I had more departmental authority. [The performing organization] doesn't take my role nearly as seriously as they should. That gets noticed by the team, and that impacts everything I do. Leading without authority gets taken to a real art form here.*"

While undoubtedly true at some organizations, it is possible that the lower authority many project managers experience is, at least partially, the result of their own misperception. The organization believes it has bestowed an adequate level of authority to match the responsibility of delivering the project. As we will see later, in Chapter Eleven, teams, organizations, and customers want leadership whether or not they explicitly ask for it, and the most successful project managers naturally grasp and exploit this fact.

Importance of Project Management

One of the attitudes that was probed by the survey was the project manager's attitude toward project management itself. Are there differences in the way Alphas and their counterparts view the profession and the value of project management?

The answer is "yes." Alphas clearly believe they can personally have a major impact on the project's success, while the non-Alphas are not always so sure. The following survey question directly probed the project manager's opinion as to the impact he or she could have on the end result. "What is the importance of your role on your current project?"

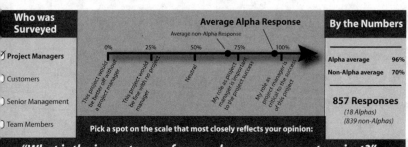

This question was designed to subjectively measure the attitude of the project manager toward his or her job. The results revealed a dramatic gap between the two groups. Nearly all of the Alphas' responses were

grouped at the extreme right end of the scale, while
the non-Alphas' responses were more varied, averaging
well above neutral, but still significantly lower in
terms of their own perceived importance and impact.

In other words, the Alphas believed in the value of
their role as project manager, while the non-Alpha
community tended to value their role far less and view
it as administrative overhead, or in the worst cases,
altogether unnecessary.

But how does the project manager's perception affect
the perception of senior management? To try and
understand that, part 2 of the Alpha Study asked
senior management to give their opinion.

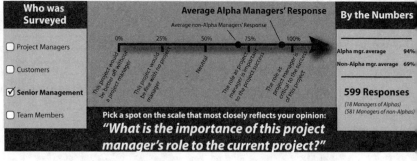

It is fascinating to consider how perception drives
reality in this case. Both the Alphas and their senior
managers perceived their role to be of the utmost
importance. The non-Alpha group, on the other hand,

believes that their role is less important, and logically, senior management agrees with them as well. While perception alone cannot make a project manager successful, the way he views his own job undoubtedly contributes to the way senior management sees it.

What The Alphas Know

Attitude is considered to be notoriously difficult to quantify. It is, by its nature, subjective; yet, when the project managers who scored in the top 2% were evaluated against the other 98%, clear differences in their attitude and approach were evident.

It became clear in the study that the Alphas were measurably more optimistic about their roles, their projects, and their careers, and this optimism was evident to teams, customers, and senior managers. One result was that they were often viewed in a more favorable light.

The Alphas are also perceived as being more professional than their counterparts by project stakeholders. The reason for this likely relates to the fact that Alphas approach their role as project manager as something valuable to the organization, important to the team, and critical to the project's success. As a whole, they treat project management as a career, which undoubtedly impacts the way they are treated by senior management as well as other stakeholders.

Noted management author, Tom Peters, once observed, *"Nobody gives you power; you just take it."* In the follow-up interviews between the Alphas and non-Alphas, it became apparent that the degree of authority a manager has on a project directly corresponds to how much authority he believes he has. Several times, the attitude was conveyed that project managers who believe they are empowered and behave accordingly usually have a greater level of authority conferred upon them than those managers who believe they lack an organizational mandate. While this approach would not apply to all organizations or all projects, it does seem to make a difference in how project managers are able to leverage the resources of the performing organization.

Finally, Alphas take the project assignment as a mandate to lead. They assume the appropriate level of authority to match their given responsibility, and they lead the project accordingly.

While attitudes and beliefs cannot by themselves explain the success enjoyed by the Alpha group, they undoubtedly provide two powerful ingredients.

Five

Focus and Prioritization

Project managers commonly complain that they feel overwhelmed by the number of things to do and the barrage of information that occurs on a project. The Alpha Study sought to understand whether the top performers in project management dealt with this problem differently than the rest of the survey population. Do they have a greater ability to manage large amounts of information, or do they have some unusual means of keeping facts and details straight?

Over 75% of the project managers who participated in The Alpha Study cited information overload as a key source of job-related stress, and the Alphas were no exception. Surprisingly, however, Alpha project managers respond to fewer e-mails per day on average than their counterparts on projects of similar size. They also spend less time in meetings than the non-Alphas; yet, senior management, teams, and customers ranked the Alphas as being more responsive to their project-related requests.

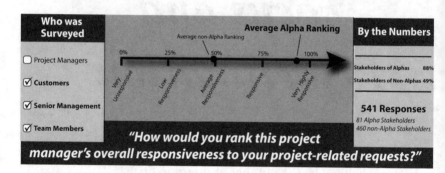

This incongruent information was first identified in the survey and explored in follow-up interviews to probe for the underlying reasons.

When asked how he dealt with the amount of information he received, Marty, an Alpha in the defense industry, stated a strategy that was prevalent among all of the Alphas when he said, "*It is pretty simple: I either manage the influx of information or it manages me, and there's not much room in between. For me it reduces down to two words: focus and prioritization.*"

Indeed, nearly all of the Alphas responded that they had formal or informal systems for maintaining focus on the project's critical success factors and for prioritizing their work.

One of the Alphas, Brandon, said, *"When I begin on a project, the first thing I do is to write down the top two or three critical success factors and post them conspicuously in a place where the team will regularly see them. We judge everything we do by those, and we make sure that everything ties back to them."*

On most projects, especially larger ones, constant influences and pressures threaten to pull the project in different directions, and it is the job of the project manager to maintain focus on the right goals and to ensure that the project is meeting those goals.

The Alphas group demonstrated two key abilities that enabled them to excel in the area of focus and prioritization.

The first ability was to sift through the massive amount of information to extract the most important components. This emerged as a life or death survival skill in project management, especially in time-critical projects. While the non-Alpha community consistently reported being overwhelmed with information and requests for information, the Alphas were able to sift out and respond to the critical elements in a timely manner.

The second ability the Alphas displayed was the ability to establish and maintain priorities on both a higher, strategic level and a lower, tactical level. The managers that made it to the Alpha group exhibited a system, formal or informal, for setting and maintaining priorities for themselves as well as each member or team.

The result of these two factors is that Alphas demonstrated the ability to create and maintain focus on the right goals and objectives more effectively than their peers. It was visible to senior management, to customers, and most saliently, to the project teams responsible for executing the work.

Sifting

Project managers are barraged by information. It comes in various forms and styles, and the volume and intensity of that information may be difficult to control. This flow of information can quickly overwhelm those who are unprepared or who have no coping strategy.

The Alpha project managers share a common skill when it comes to sifting through the inflow of information in that they learn to intuit. In other words, although they may not have a formal system for deciding which information is important and which is not, they develop the ability to cull out the most important aspects of the project, much like a physician learns to detect cues and subtleties invisible to most people.

Renowned University of Chicago psychologist, and chair of the Drucker School, Dr. Mihaly Csikszentmihalyi, estimates that, on average, we are bombarded by some 4,082,400 "bits" of information in a working day. Of course, not all of these are fully processed, but this information assails our senses. The sources for this information would include pieces of conversations we overhear but may not pay attention to, stray noises, discussions, feelings of hunger or desire, our sense of the temperature in the room, expressions on a co-worker's face, or a ringing phone.

The good news is that the human mind is quite adept at navigating this continuous river of information to know what to pay attention to and what to ignore, and most of this is done on a subconscious level. This process continues while you sleep, where your brain may choose to ignore the sound of a car passing by your home, but may rouse you at the sound of a crying child or a barking dog. While this is true at a mundane level, as is illustrated by the preceding examples, it is also true at the level of job performance.

When asked to count the number of daily non-SPAM e-mail messages received over the preceding 28 day period, the total average for all project managers was 119 per day, with a few skewing the distribution at 250+. There is generally a strong correlation between the number of active stakeholders and the number of e-mail messages received, although this may be

influenced by other factors, such as a distributed
workforce, network infrastructure, or corporate
culture.

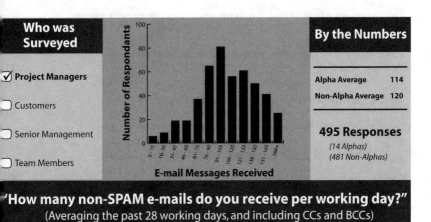

Who was Surveyed

☑ **Project Managers**

❏ Customers

❏ Senior Management

❏ Team Members

Number of Respondents

100
80
60
40
20
0

0–15 16–30 31–45 46–60 61–75 76–90 91–105 106–120 121–135 136–150 151–165 166+

E-mail Messages Received

By the Numbers

Alpha Average   114

Non-Alpha Average   120

495 Responses
(14 Alphas)
(481 Non-Alphas)

"How many non-SPAM e-mails do you receive per working day?"
(Averaging the past 28 working days, and including CCs and BCCs)

For managers of larger, international projects,
this electronic onslaught of information became
particularly brutal, continuing 24 hours per day.
When asked how they manage this influx of electronic
communication, the responses of the top project
managers and those at the bottom showed some
striking differences.

Consider Jeff, a non-Alpha project manager with two
years experience, who placed in the bottom third of
all of the survey participants. *"Over the past month, I
received nearly 150 e-mail messages every working day. I*

would put out one fire, only to find that another, larger one had popped up. Some days I am certain that all I did was reply to e-mail, but if I ignore them the phone starts ringing off the hook, or worse yet, my manager's phone will start ringing."

Contrast that with Melinda, an Alpha project manager who ranked near the top of every metric. When asked the same question, she responded, *"E-mail is one of my biggest potential distractions. I could easily spend my whole day on nothing but e-mail, but I wouldn't get real work done."*

This contradistinction between a non-Alpha and an Alpha mirrors a common thread that runs through the overall population. The belief that responding to e-mail does not generally constitute "real work" is a belief that pervades the Alpha group. They do not manage projects via e-mail, and they do not let others manage their agenda via e-mail. Instead of responding to every e-mail as it flows into their inbox, the Alphas typically respond in batches, one to three times per day.

Along these same lines, portable devices that deliver
e-mail were slightly less common among the Alpha
group. In the Alpha group, 24% carried an e-mail-
enabled device such as an ultraportable, a PDA or
an e-mail enabled cell phone, while 36% of the
non-Alpha group carried these devices. While still
a low number relative to the overall population of
project managers, the number is 50% higher for the
non-Alpha community, and this ratio is indicative of
the attitude that e-mail is there to serve the project
manager and not vice versa.

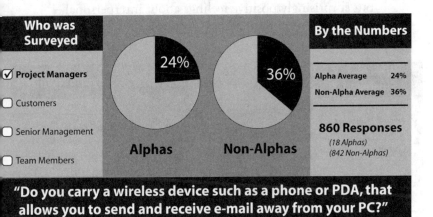

Who was Surveyed

☑ **Project Managers**

◯ Customers

◯ Senior Management

◯ Team Members

24%   **Alphas**   36%   **Non-Alphas**

By the Numbers

Alpha Average	24%
Non-Alpha Average	36%

860 Responses
(18 Alphas)
(842 Non-Alphas)

"Do you carry a wireless device such as a phone or PDA, that allows you to send and receive e-mail away from your PC?"

Meetings were another form of informational
onslaught, presenting a genuine threat to many
project managers resulting in lost time. Jim, a non-
Alpha project manager at an insurance company in
Ohio said, "*Meetings have turned out to be a significant*

challenge for me. I typically spend half my workweek in
meetings, which wastes a lot of time. It's a real challenge.
If I attend, I waste time, but I can't risk missing
something important."

When asked to log the time they spent in meetings
of any kind over the course of a month, a telling fact
emerged. The non-Alpha group logged 25% more
time in meetings of three or more people. Follow-up
interviews with the Alpha group produced similar,
generally negative feelings about larger meetings,
but surprisingly positive feelings about interpersonal
communication.

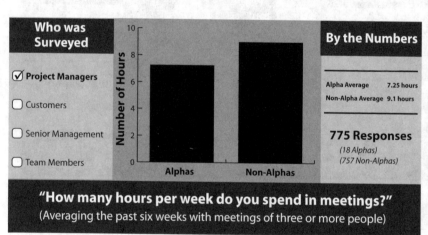

Who was Surveyed

☑ Project Managers
☐ Customers
☐ Senior Management
☐ Team Members

Number of Hours — Alphas / Non-Alphas

By the Numbers

Alpha Average   7.25 hours
Non-Alpha Average   9.1 hours

775 Responses
(18 Alphas)
(757 Non-Alphas)

"How many hours per week do you spend in meetings?"
(Averaging the past six weeks with meetings of three or more people)

Victor, an Alpha project manager at a consulting firm,
expressed, "*I much prefer to speak with someone in*
person than over the phone or e-mail. I can accomplish

so much more that way, and I don't have to worry about
things getting misconstrued or taken out of context. If the
conversation was very delicate or important I will almost
always follow it up with an e-mail, but it will only be a
short recap of what was decided."

In the interviews, many of the non-Alpha managers,
particularly in the bottom quintile, gave the
impression of being like a radio, bombarded by
static, but unable to tune in to a single frequency.
Under siege by bits of work-related and personal
information, they finally resorted to tuning in and
responding to whatever sounded the most urgent. Yet
even though these project managers made the effort
to answer their e-mail more quickly than the Alphas,
they were rated as being less responsive to stakeholder
needs than their top counterparts. More of the
underlying reasons for this finding are explored in the
next chapter.

Setting and Maintaining Priorities

Once the Alpha group has sifted through information
to locate the relevant pieces of information, they must
set priorities.

According to several Alphas, this ability to prioritize is most important early in the project. Brenda, an Alpha in the soft drink industry says, *"I set the project's priorities early on, and I post them on the wall where no one can miss them. If anyone has any doubts about what we're supposed to be doing, all they have to do is look. I make sure my manager, the customer, and other senior stakeholders are in agreement before I actually post the priorities, and those usually don't change throughout the project."*

When interviewed in greater depth, Alphas showed common characteristics in setting priorities. They tended to divide their priorities into two main categories. The first category was higher-level or strategic priorities, tied to the critical success factors (CSFs) and primary constraints of the project.

These strategic categories, or meta-goals, tended to be tied to higher level concerns that would make or break the entire project. Much like the famous, "It's the economy, stupid," that framed Clinton's presidential campaign, these "meta-goals" give structure and overarching purpose to the project.

Strategic priorities, as Brenda indicated, typically remain static throughout the project. If a change were made to one of these goals, it would represent a major change to the project, and perhaps a full evaluation of whether the project should be continued in its current form.

Tactical priorities, on the other hand, regularly change. Sudhir, an Alpha with a retail company in the Northeastern United States, said, *"My [tactical] priorities are tied to the execution of the ongoing work. Every Friday, I prioritize the work for the following week. The projects I manage are so technical that we often cannot plan in detail more than two or three weeks ahead, since we don't know what technical obstacles we will run into. The big picture probably won't change for us, but the step-by-step of how we get there almost certainly will."*

This ability to prioritize becomes an ongoing task. Priorities are set and reevaluated at regular intervals. The tactical priorities drive the work, while the strategic priorities drive the tactical. The big picture is established early on and rarely changes.

When probed further, it was discovered that 83% of the Alpha group had a deliberate system for the regular prioritization of goals and work plans. Some of these systems were as simple as a weekly note on a calendar that served as a reminder for them to reevaluate priorities, while others set aside an hour early in the morning on a particular day of the week (typically Monday or Wednesday) to set priorities. This prioritization was done without distraction or outside influence.

What the Alphas Know

The sheer volume of information that most project managers receive threatens to disrupt the project manager's ability to carry out his job. Being able to sift through information and cull out the most important pieces is an essential survival skill for Alpha project managers. They are able to deftly navigate which meetings and conference calls to attend, which e-mails require a response, and how to maximize their stakeholder responsiveness. Much of this is done by setting up the right systems and categories and sorting the information appropriately. The Alphas made it clear that the same system did not always work from one project to the next. Instead, they tailored the categories and methods used to the project.

When looking at the questions the survey asked, it would be rational to assume that the project managers would either rank high on internal facing (i.e. responsive to team needs or responsive to senior management requests), or external facing (i.e. responsive to external stakeholder requests). However, the Alphas seemed to defy this prediction. The Alpha project managers consistently scored above their peers on both internal and external responsiveness.

Six

Communication

Of all the attributes that separate the Alpha group from their peers, communication presents the most striking difference. The primary reason for this difference is that the average project manager does not always have an accurate handle on his or her own communication skills or effectiveness.

It has been estimated that project managers spend 90% of their working time communicating in one form or another. This estimate is less arresting when one considers that it includes status reports, meetings, memos, e-mail, voice mail, and other formal and informal discussions. The act of communicating overlaps many other areas and permeates most of the activities project managers perform. For instance, a two-hour planning meeting could be thought of as planning, but it also likely constitutes a legitimate communication activity.

When non-Alpha project managers were asked to rank their personal communication effectiveness on a linear scale from 1 to 100, the project managers scored themselves, on average, at 82%.

When the Alphas are separated out from the other project managers, they rank themselves similarly on communication effectiveness, ticking up only two percentage points. This similarity invited further inquiry. Are Alphas better communicators than their peers, or do both groups actually perform similarly?

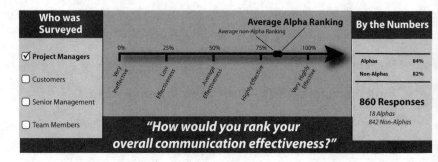

To answer this, both the Alpha and non-Alpha groups further analyzed; however, instead of only talking to the project managers, the survey looked outward to

include their teams, customers, and senior managers.
When these stakeholder groups were surveyed and
asked how the project managers performed, their
responses diverged sharply from those of most of the
project managers.

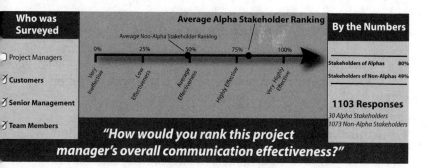

Throughout this book, areas of disconnect between
project managers and their stakeholders raise potential
cause for concern, and no greater gap was found than
this one. An astonishing 94% of all project managers
gave themselves a more favorable ranking when it
came to communication than their stakeholders did.
This phenomenon extended to project managers
across all industries, and encompassed both Alphas
and non-Alphas.

To understand the underlying causes of this
gap, both the project managers and stakeholders

were interviewed regarding project-related communications. After conducting nearly sixty of these interviews, it became apparent that the vast majority of project managers lack two key communication skills.

Probing Expectations

First, many project managers lack a key understanding of their audience's communication needs. Even those managers (including the Alphas) who formally surveyed their stakeholders in advance to understand their communication requirements did not always seem to fully grasp stakeholder expectations.

Lori, an Alpha from the strategic outsourcing industry said, "*If a waiter asks me how I want my meal prepared, I'm going to pay more attention when my meal comes to the table. When a project manager asks me what information I need to see while the project is in progress, I'm going to be very interested to see if he listened to what I said.*"

In other words, asking and not listening can be worse than not asking at all. By asking for input, the project manager creates an expectation with the stakeholders that the input matters.

Seeking Feedback

The other skill that project managers typically lack is an awareness of how their communication was being received by the stakeholder. In other words, project managers did not have an understanding of the effect their communication was having. Even the ones that were dutiful about distributing information they felt was relevant usually did not understand how that information was received or interpreted on behalf of the stakeholders.

Typical project managers will gravitate toward communicating the information they want people to know, with little understanding of the real needs and expectations of the audience. When probed on why they communicated the information they did, most indicated that they based their communication on their experience. In other words, they felt that their communication had been adequate in the past, and so they continued to build on what they felt was an overall pattern of success.

While the Alpha project managers exhibited many of the same behaviors as the non-Alphas when it came to communication, it should also be noted that, as a group, they outperformed the non-Alphas by 31% as ranked by their stakeholders.

The 18 Alphas were then interviewed in depth to try and understand the techniques and practices they employed when communicating with stakeholders. Through these interviews, four common Alpha traits emerged. While none of these techniques are unusual when viewed alone, their frequent occurrence in the top performers is noteworthy.

These top four traits are:

1. The Alphas talk to stakeholders very early in the project to understand their audience's requests and tailor communication to meet their needs.

2. The Alphas set a communication schedule, and adhere to it stringently.

3. The Alphas communicate their message in a clear and concise manner, without wasting time.

4. The Alphas create an open channel, regularly
   dialoguing with stakeholders about the
   communication itself.

These four traits are explored in the remainder of this
chapter.

Understand

According to Melinda, an Alpha who works in
technology outsourcing, "Communication is my
customer service, and it has to be market-driven." In
other words, the project manager must determine
what the stakeholders want and need to know and
customize project communications to be on target.
This attitude was reiterated throughout interviews
with the Alpha group.

Knowing your audience is absolutely critical to your
success as a communicator.

Jim, an Alpha in a manufacturing company, shared his
approach. "*Rather than try to interview every individual
stakeholder, I group them together – especially on larger
projects. I get at least one representative from each*

group to give me input on the group's communication requirements, and I give everyone a chance to evaluate the results before anything is finalized."

Jim continues, *"Every group has unique communication requirements. For instance, [my PMO] will typically want weekly updates, while our production department may only need monthly updates, but that is up to them to decide."*

Be Predictable

Another key trait shared by the Alpha group was that they adhered to a strict communications schedule.

Consider Brenda, who made a predictable schedule a top priority. In one post-survey interview, her manager shared that she typically distributed a weekly status report via e-mail at 8:00 a.m. every Friday. One Friday, however, he received the status report at precisely 8:00 a.m. when he knew she was on an international trip without Internet access. Brenda had prepared the report in advance, and rather than distribute it the night before, she scheduled her e-mail system to send it at precisely 8:00 a.m.

While this was an unusual example of dedication to time and schedule, it was not the only one. Alphas put a premium on regular and predictable communication, and they used this technique to manage stakeholder expectations.

Thomas, an Alpha in information technology said, "*This really gets to the heart of how I cut down on individual requests. After about the first month of the project, people know when they can expect communication from me and the format it will follow. I try to take the mystery out of that right from the start. People are less likely to bombard me with unnecessary e-mail requests if they know they'll get their questions answered once a week in my standard communication to them and they know they can count on it being there.*"

Hand in hand with predictability is consistency. One of the most frequent stakeholder complaints that emerged during interviews was that communication from the project manager was often sporadic and irregular. It seems that inconsistent and unpredictable communication did as much or more harm as no communication at all.

Terence, a senior manager of two non-Alphas had strong words to say about the inconsistent communication he receives. "*I never know what to expect from [these two]. If I get consistent communication – even if it is consistently bad – that is something I can work with. At least I know where to start, but when it is this intermittent, then I am never really sure what to expect. I'm starting to wonder if a stable format and a quick spell check are too much to ask?*"

To understand how the Alphas deal with this, consider Brenda's approach. "*I send out a regular status to three different groups of users each week via e-mail. Most of the information is actually the same, but it is tailored to the audience, and I use basically the same format for most of my projects. I make them short and to the point. I post these reports online at 8:00 a.m. every Friday, and the portal we use automatically e-mails the stakeholders that a new report has been posted.*"

Consistent and predictable communication requires it to be elevated to a top priority. It means that in order to rise to the top of the field, project managers must commit to letting their stakeholders know information, whether positive or negative, at precisely the agreed-upon time. If the information was not available at that time, the project manager must post the report anyway, alert stakeholders to the omission, and specify when an update is expected.

Clarify and Simplify

The top project managers are masters of the obvious: simple and effective communication. They communicate the right information, and they communicate it well. In addition to being consistent, effective project communication is clear, complete, and concise.

When stakeholders were interviewed regarding how clear and concise project communications were, they often erupted in frustration. One team member of a non-Alpha stated, "*I used to read [the project manager's] e-mails and status reports, but I don't waste my time anymore. They ramble on for pages about everything except what her team cares about. If I need to know something, I usually ask my technical lead, or as a last resort, I pick up the phone and call [the project manager]."*

A senior manager at a large outsourcing company took steps to address this issue within her organization. "*I could not believe how poorly my project managers and business analysts wrote. We all took a business writing class together, and that did seem to improve things, but we still have a long way to go. I am one of those people who just can't get past run-on sentences and glaring grammatical errors.*"

When stakeholders were asked to comment specifically on the clarity and conciseness of the project manager's communication to them, several discernible traits were identified. When communication lacked conciseness and clarity, stakeholders were more likely to want to replace the project manager.

Frustration was only slightly improved when the communication was clear, but the communication was very wordy, lengthy, or too frequent. As one customer of a non-Alpha put it, "*I don't have time to read the volume of material this project manager expects me to. A lot of the time, it feels like I'm drinking from the proverbial fire hose. When I mentioned [to the project manager] that I didn't have time to read everything he was sending me, his response to me was, 'You should.*'"

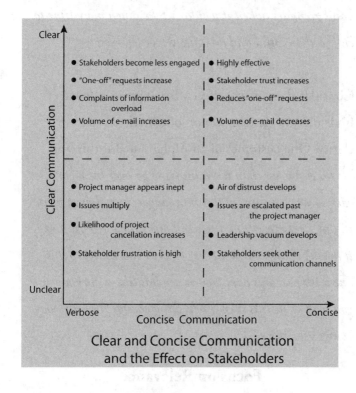

**Clear and Concise Communication
and the Effect on Stakeholders**

Perhaps the worst scenario is when the communication is concise and unclear. Stakeholders are forced to find other ways to get their information. Consider one stakeholder of a non-Alpha from a call center management company. "*We've had this problem many times in the past where the project manager sends out these two sentence e-mails that send people running for cover. Last month one person resigned because they (incorrectly) thought they were being let go. Too many project managers in our organization lob e-mails like hand grenades, when it wouldn't take much more time to craft a thoughtful and accurately-worded message."*

Consider the positive effect when a project manager finds that magic intersection of conciseness and clarity. One customer of an Alpha stated it this way. *"It takes me less than ten minutes to go over his reports each week. I'm sure it takes him longer than that to write it, but I get everything I need in one simple report, and it doesn't change format every week. I can compare this one with previous ones, and it unfolds like a story when you look at it. It is such a refreshing change from the way things used to be."*

Focus on Relevance

The Alpha group also put a premium on communicating relevant information to stakeholders.

Jeff, an Alpha in software development, commented on the importance of sending the right message to the right stakeholders. *"It would be a disaster for me to share the same information with my customer that I share with my team. I manage the communications very carefully on my project. Most things never need to make it to my boss or my customer."*

Lori is an Alpha for a large retailer whose stakeholders raved without reservation about her effective communication. She shared this approach to making sure her message is relevant. "*I learned three things early in my career from a fantastic project manager who mentored and trained me:*

> "*I always provide a very brief summary of the information I am communicating up front. I go on to include supporting information and supplemental data if necessary.*

> "*I find out what measurements are of interest to my group, and I always include these in my communication.*

> "*I try to keep things very crisp. I don't ever bombard people with information for information's sake. I believe it's my job to draw conclusions, and I'm not afraid to do that.*"

Fear of Communication

One of the common complaints of the non-Alpha group was that communicating opens the project manager up to a host of potential issues. Knowledge is power. Hostile stakeholders may use information to further their own agendas instead of supporting the project.

Michael, a non-Alpha project manager, put it this way. *"I realize I'm probably not the strongest communicator, but in my organization, you get beat up more for what you say than for what you don't say."* Others also echoed this sentiment. Communicating a plan is often seen as limiting the project manager's options, and written communication provides a baseline against which the project manager may be measured.

Several of the project managers who participated in the study communicated that they feel pressure to agree to overly optimistic targets early in the project. Taking this "easy way out" in early stages of the project, however, can have the unanticipated side effect of making communication more difficult in later project phases. As one of the Alphas, Dan, put it, *"No one likes to communicate bad news. If the project starts off working toward an unrealistic goal, then almost all communication from that point forward is guaranteed to be bad."*

What The Alphas Know

On many projects, communication is the only
deliverable the stakeholders will have up until the
time the product is completed. This concept may
explain why so many projects are canceled before
a product, service, or result is ever produced. The
communication was poor, and the project was canned.

Statistically, project communications is the one
area identified in this study with the single greatest
gap between the Alphas and non-Alphas. Not only
is there a wide disparity between the two groups,
but even the Alphas scored a disappointing 80% in
effectiveness when evaluated by their stakeholders.
Still, the Alphas as a group were largely praised for
their communication.

The greatest disconnect between the two groups
seemed to be that the Alphas were generally aware of
how their message was being received by stakeholders,
while the non-Alphas seemed either unaware of or
disinterested in the effect of their communication.
Alphas took the time to understand stakeholder needs
in advance, and they tailored communication to meet
those needs.

The Alpha group made reliable and predictable communications a priority, even going so far as using this as a tool to manage stakeholders. By communicating predictably with their stakeholders, they were able to reduce many requests for information, and by doing so regularly, they built trust.

While stakeholders often expressed frustration with the non-Alpha group when it came to effective communication, the Alphas excelled in this area. Communication that was neither concise nor clear caused stakeholders to feel disconnected from the project and to search for unofficial communication channels to satisfy their needs. Alphas, on the other hand, set the gold standard here by making their information not only very clear and highly concise, but also relevant to their audience. Stakeholders were given the information that was important to them because their needs were clearly understood.

But perhaps most important of all was the deceptively simple fact that Alpha project managers do communicate. They made it a top priority to communicate, whether it was good news or bad, and regardless of whether it was convenient for them to do so.

Seven α

Approach

This chapter investigates the similarities and differences between the Alpha and non-Alpha groups in approaching a project. Specifically, it looks at the roles the project managers fill, and how much time they spend performing various project tasks. One of the most curious findings in this section was the gap that existed between what project managers believe (or say they believe) and their actions. This was especially evident in the area of the project manager's approach to the project.

As discussed in Chapter Two, the study on the project managers themselves was divided into three parts. The first was a survey that sought out characteristics, and the second was a follow-up survey that delved deeper into the underlying factors and motivations behind those characteristics. The third component was phone interviews to probe certain aspects in more detail.

In part one of the survey, project managers were asked to specify their approach to project management, and few deviated from variants of Deming's "Plan, Do, Check, Act" approach popularized in the 1950s. Some project managers articulated this cycle as "planning, executing, monitoring, and controlling," but the overall approach was highly similar. The project manager planned the work, the team performed the work, the project manager evaluated the work, and corrective action was taken when necessary.

In fact, with the uncanny similarity in responses among the survey participants, it was uncertain whether there would be any difference between the Alpha and non-Alpha groups when it came to how they approached the project.

The Importance Of Planning

In part one of the survey, participants were asked how important careful pre-execution project planning was to their efforts and to quantify their response

on a linear scale from 1 to 100. The results were
indistinguishable between the two groups. Both the
Alphas and the non-Alphas ranked the importance
of project planning nearly as high as the survey
allowed. Practically all of the participants responded
that careful planning prior to execution was crucial
to overall project success, and several accompanying
comments stressed that this was the key the project
manager used to manage everything from acceptance
to expectations to team morale.

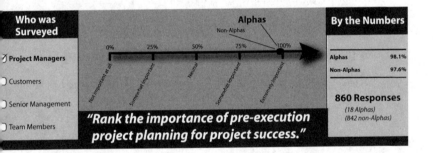

While the aforementioned results were not overly
surprising, they begged more exploration in part two
of the survey. Now that the project manager's belief
in the importance of planning had been established,
why not try to see if their actual practice reflected that
belief?

In part two of the survey, participants were asked to specify the amount of time they allocated to activities in the five accepted project management process groups (Initiating, Planning, Executing, Controlling, and Closing) on all projects they had managed over the previous three years. The goal of this question was to investigate whether Alphas allocate their time and the energies of their teams differently on projects than do non-Alphas.

As a starting point, survey participants were asked to categorize the labor hours their team had spent on these projects and to express each process group sub-total as a percent of the overall total. This would give a ratio that could be compared against the other participants. It should be noted that although results were originally segregated by length of time, size of budget, and industry, there were no discernible differences among large and small projects or among industries, and so the results were aggregated for this analysis.

Although Alphas and non-Alphas ranked the importance of planning roughly the same, in practice,

Alphas allocated just over twice as much time toward project planning as their counterparts. In fact, the Alpha group reported spending more time in every process group except for execution. When one considers the fact that most of a typical project's labor hours, cost, and resources are expended in project execution activities, the implications on schedule and budget are clear. Although both groups maintain that they are equally committed to project planning, it is difficult not to conclude that the Alphas execute more efficiently by planning more thoroughly.

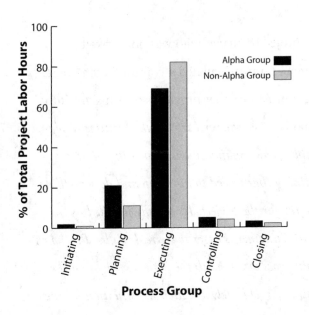

Who was Surveyed	Process Group	Alphas	Non-Alphas	By the Numbers
☑ Project Managers	Initiating	2%	1%	
	Planning	21%	11%	**365 Responses**
☐ Customers	Executing	69%	82%	15 Alphas
☐ Senior Management	Controlling	5%	4%	350 non-Alphas
☐ Team Members	Closing	3%	2%	

Actual % of Project Labor Hours Allocated to Each Process Group
(Includes projects managed over the previous three consecutive years)

Although far from conclusive, this finding hints at the fact that more actual planning may be good up to a point. Both groups seem aware of this finding, but there is a cognitive dissonance at work among the non-Alpha group in this regard.

Jerry, a project manager who was not ranked in the Alpha group, articulated a common complaint among non-Alphas that provides some insight into his response. *"Whenever I try to take the time to plan, inevitably [senior management] comes in and starts complaining that I need to hurry up and do something 'productive' for the project. It's usually justified by saying the customer is eager to see real results. But when something goes wrong with the plan, I'm right on the firing line. It's definitely a 'Catch 22' situation for the team."*

So although he personally ranked the importance
of planning at 100, Jerry felt that he was unable to
allocate the number of planning hours that the project
required.

Another area of approach that the survey probed was
the role the project manager should play. Should
the project manager only manage, or should he
share responsibility for technical aspects? While it
is understood that one approach does not work for
all projects, the goal of the survey was to evaluate
what kind of work the project managers were
performing and what was expected of them by senior
management.

"Hands-On Project Management"

Participants were asked how "hands-on" the project
manager should be. In other words, is it best for a
project manager to confine his or her duties to pure
project management across one or more projects,
or is it best for a project manager to also be actively
involved in the technical work of the project?

When presented with this question, both groups answered similarly, indicating that their direct involvement in project execution is a factor of the team that they have in place and the size of the project. A strong majority of project managers expressed a preference for a pure project management role; however, as we will see, that is not necessarily aligned with senior management's expectations.

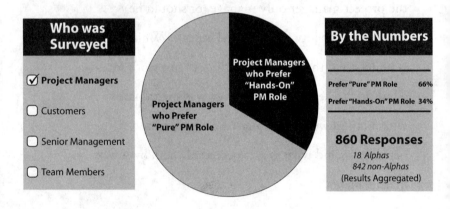

Who was Surveyed

- ☑ Project Managers
- ☐ Customers
- ☐ Senior Management
- ☐ Team Members

Project Managers who Prefer "Hands-On" PM Role

Project Managers who Prefer "Pure" PM Role

By the Numbers

Prefer "Pure" PM Role   66%

Prefer "Hands-On" PM Role   34%

860 Responses
18 Alphas
842 non-Alphas
(Results Aggregated)

One of the responses that was in the minority came from Jeff, an Alpha at a commercial software development house, who described his project involvement this way: "*Before I became a project manager, I spent over 20 years in software development, so I still enjoy wading into the code from time to time. It seems to be a big trend today for project managers to manage outside of their domain, but I find [my domain expertise] to be a critical advantage, and I enjoy being hands-on.*"

While Jeff's comments don't match the sentiments of most project managers, they do reflect the views of senior management. A full 78% of senior managers who responded to this question indicated that they preferred that the project manager have some technical involvement or responsibility. In other words, organizations largely prefer that project managers do more than pure project management, even when the project manager is responsible for more than one project at a time.

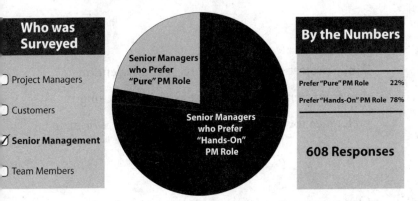

Subject Matter Expertise

Another topic raised by many project managers in survey comments was the value of domain expertise. Is a project manager who is an expert in the project's product inherently more valuable than someone who is "domain independent" but has strong project management expertise? Survey participants were sharply divided on this subject. Many advocated subject matter expertise as crucial to effective management of the project, while others posited that a domain-independent project manager could be more effective.

The project management community was divided on this issue, but how did organizations feel? Was domain expertise preferable? If so, how important was it?

While project managers are largely ambivalent on this point, senior management expressed a strong preference toward project managers who were domain experts.

One senior manager who was also the head of the organization's project management office expressed her view. "*There have been some groups who have pushed us to embrace domain-independence in our project managers, and there has been a lot of hype surrounding the claim that a domain-independent project manager could do a better job than a domain expert, but I don't buy it. Surely they don't believe that domain neutrality is better for all management disciplines or that project management is unique in this regard? We have a highly specialized product and a highly specialized methodology, and for someone to come in and have to learn both from the ground up would be a real disadvantage for everyone. I've personally observed a direct link between the amount of domain expertise and the project manager's time-to-value. If there is an objective disadvantage to having a domain expert as the project manager, I can't imagine what it would be."*

To understand this finding in more detail, part two of the survey asked project managers to report on how often they worked in a domain where they had expertise.

"Over the past five years, on what percentage of projects that you managed did you have domain expertise when you began the project?"

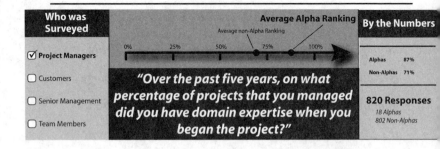

It should be noted that both groups work on projects where they have product expertise far more often than not, so to continue this line of questioning, project managers were also asked about their opinion of domain expertise, and here, a key difference in attitude emerged. Alphas believed far more often than non-Alphas that domain expertise was an important contributing factor to their success on the project.

All project managers who participated in the survey were asked: "Rank the importance of the project manager being a domain expert as a contributor to overall project success."

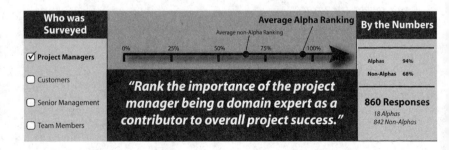

This surprising gap touches on a larger debate within the project management community, but the overall responses here indicate that senior managers and the Alpha community believe that subject matter expertise on the project's product does add value and that being a project manager is not always enough by itself.

Sarah, an Alpha project manager in the telecommunications industry, commented on how she generally filled more than one project role. "*I can't make a blanket statement about value and productivity when it comes to a dedicated project manager. I worked on a recent project that was very large, and I was dedicated as the full-time project manager. This project needed a full-time project manager, but the one I am on today really doesn't. I'm filling the roles of project manager, business analyst, and technical writer. It wouldn't make sense for me to be dedicated full-time only to project management, because after the project plan was rolled out, I would have a lot of free time on my hands.*"

One senior manager from a Fortune 500 company expressed his attitude on the issue. "*We have nearly*

1,000 project managers in our division alone, and I would venture that there are less than twenty that only manage, and the ones that are dedicated project managers will generally manage more than one project at a time. We value multi-disciplinary teams, and one person may fill several project roles. We've experimented with this quite a bit, and I can say from experience that [one person filling more than one project role] just works better. It preserves continuity when turnover hits, and when everyone wears multiple hats, it flattens out the team, which fits our culture."

What The Alphas Know

It would be premature to conclude that Alphas know that planning is more important than the non-Alphas. When both groups were interviewed and their attitudes were explored, they both spoke passionately about how planning must precede execution. Why then, did the Alphas plan for over twice as many hours relative to the project length? Perhaps the question should be "how?" It is likely that at least some of the answer lies in the fact that both groups wanted to plan for an extended length of time, but only the Alphas were able to do this. This could be because of the organizational support and trust the Alphas had, or the fact that they were able to "sell" extensive planning to their customer and organization.

As a group, the Alphas also knew that most organizations prefer hands-on project managers. While many resist a split role, or reject it outright as lacking in focus, the Alphas are playing multiple roles on the project, usually keeping their hands deep in the construction of the product.

Alphas have been in their current job an average of nearly two years longer than the non-Alphas, and the domain expertise that accompanies their tenure certainly counts in the eyes of senior management. While debate continues as to whether a manager should ideally be a subject matter expert, or should be more abstracted from the technical aspects of the project, the Alphas are silently punching their ballots in favor of deep domain and product expertise.

Eight

Relationships and Conflict

Conflict has been labeled "a growth industry," and one need not spend much time in politics or the corporate world before that opinion is validated.

One dimension that the Alpha survey sought to measure was how project managers dealt with conflict on their projects. An interesting aspect of this study was that it did not rely on one stakeholder or even on one group of stakeholders. It included the customer, who was often external to the organization; senior management, almost always internal to the organization; and the team members, who often had their own departmental, external, or independent loyalties.

Having to satisfy all of these groups in addition to accomplishing the project objectives made becoming an Alpha particularly challenging. The survey results were filled with project managers who had the unquestioned support and admiration of their team, but were roundly disliked by their senior managers, or project managers who were loved by their customers but whose teams were on the brink of mutiny, begging for another person to lead the project.

Satisfying various stakeholder concerns is at the heart of the project management challenge, and only rarely do all project stakeholders have identical visions or goals for the same project. In fact, it is much more likely for a project ma nager to face a scenario where the stakeholders have competing or even conflicting goals. One functional manager may welcome the accuracy and speed provided by a new robotic assembly system, while another may hold deep concern of how this will affect his department's head count. Even in organizations with strong vertical alignment, there often exists a classic tension between departments, such as operations and business development, marketing and engineering, or product implementation and product support. Much of this organizational tension often comes to a point of intense focus on the project, where concepts are being implemented, and no one feels that tension more than the project manager.

Balancing competing or conflicting goals with the overall satisfaction of the stakeholders is at the heart of project management, which inevitably uncovers or produces conflict. This task requires the project manager to combine the empirical and analytical skills often associated with project management with strong leadership, and with softer skills such as persuasion, negotiation, compromise, and conflict resolution. As conflict increases, relationship management becomes one of the project manager's most crucial tasks. Without this skill, projects typically experience ever-increasing turbulence until the project is canceled, the project manager is fired, or outside parties are brought in to "rescue" the project.

The Challenge Of Consensus

Helping disparate groups with varying goals reach consensus is one of the most difficult tasks a project manager faces. The customer may want what is perceived as the most cost-effective solution for her company, while the team responsible for execution may want to do what is easiest. An organization's marketing group may want to reuse existing components to leverage previous investments, while research and development may want to create entirely new components based on the latest technology. When all of these innumerable potentialities converge upon the project manager, a solution may seem nonexistent.

As Abraham Lincoln noted, "*You cannot please all of the people all of the time.*"

In the course of interviews, project managers who ranked in the lowest third on the composite Alpha index expressed considerable frustration on the point of reaching consensus. One of these managers summed up the attitudes of many when he said, "*Getting everyone to agree on the outcome is next to impossible. Everyone approaches [this project] with their own agenda, and their only goal seems to be to get me to accept their agenda and just ignore everyone else.*"

Multiply that scenario by numerous stakeholders, and the dilemma becomes clear. This explains, in part, why the non-Alpha project managers found it particularly difficult to create consensus on projects. When senior managers, customers, and teams were asked whether the project manager was able to manage the project in such a way that their goals were satisfied, the difference was notable.

For the purposes of the Alpha survey, consensus was defined as follows: "*Getting the relevant stakeholders to agree to support the decision, even if they do not necessarily agree with the decision itself.*"

But before a stakeholder's goals can be met or satisfied, they must be understood. If a stakeholder's goals are not understood, they will not be met except by random chance.

The following question was posed to over 1,100 stakeholders: "How would you rate this project manager's ability to identify, understand, and satisfy your individual goals for the project?"

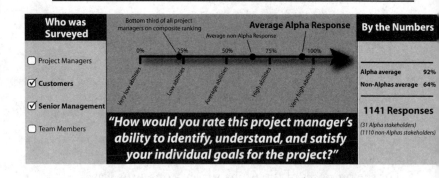

Although the average non-Alpha ranked above 50%, the bottom third of the composite Alpha index of project managers showed particularly low rankings on this score. Considering only the project managers that ranked in the bottom 33% on the composite score (the same score that determined who was an Alpha), the average ranking was a depressing 23% at their ability to satisfy stakeholder goals.

Thomas, an Alpha who manages a commercial software application said, *"Consensus is the holy grail of project management. You can usually detect the fault lines as soon as you start putting the requirements down in writing. But if you plow ahead without getting everyone to generally agree, you are begging for trouble."*

Relationships

During post-survey interviews with the two groups, another discernible trend began to emerge. The recurring theme of the Alpha group was that they relied on an informal network to accomplish formal project activities rather than only on their assigned teams, while non-Alphas gravitated toward using only defined channels to accomplish project work. In other words, an Alpha was more likely to use someone not explicitly assigned to his project than a non-Alpha was in order to complete project work. One possible reason for this is that Alphas tend to build extensive networks within their organization, and they will use these networks to solve problems, or to streamline bureaucratic procedures that have the potential to slow the project down. For example, Kyle, a project manager from the Alpha group, had a strong relationship with the Chief Information Officer in his organization that went back several years. When the functional manager would not grant him access to a particular data warehouse he needed in a timely manner, he used his relationship with the CIO to accelerate the process and keep his original timeline intact.

Kyle explained it this way. *"Relationships are like muscles. You have to use them in order for them to get stronger. I didn't approach this as if I were asking [the CIO] for a favor. I felt like I was helping the organization by keeping an important project on track, and ultimately that's my job. He understood that. If I had approached this like I wanted to force an issue to a head and try and pull rank, I would still be waiting for access to those databases. This way, all of the relationships were strengthened, or at least preserved, by the time this was over."*

For Alphas, informal networks often take on far more importance than the formal organizational networks. The larger the organization, the more pronounced this tendency becomes. This is not to imply that project managers are necessarily iconoclasts or bureaucracy-haters. Instead, they use the organizational hierarchy to their advantage instead of allowing it to unfavorably constrain their project.

Brandon, an Alpha in the commercial airline industry, cited the importance of using informal networks. *"About three years ago, I was assigned my largest project to date, which was the redesign of a section of the*

*empennage on a commercial aircraft, and there were
an unbelievable number of things to think about. I
spent most of my time worrying that I was going to miss
something critical. Then one afternoon, an idea hit me,
and I left work early and went to see a guy who had done
this job for almost 20 years before me. I had never met
him, but I called and asked if I could come by. He was
retired, and we spent the afternoon at his home, talking.
He wasn't a resource assigned to my team, but the time
spent was more valuable than I could have imagined."*

Dave, an Alpha in the insurance industry, said this
about his network of professional relationships. "*I
make it a point never to burn bridges with coworkers. I
started my career in the mid-1970s, and I still keep in
touch with a lot of the people I worked with back then.
I've relied on that group when I was unemployed in the
1980s and overcoming cancer in the 1990s, and my
relationships with them today are stronger than ever.*"

Conflict

Another component of the survey focused on the
project manager's ability to resolve conflict. When
stakeholders were asked to rank the project manager's
performance on conflict resolution, the composite
results were markedly low, even for the Alpha group.

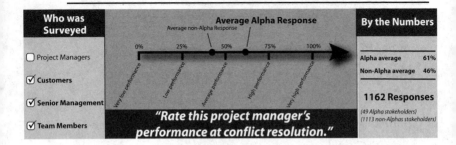

One senior manager at a telecommunications consulting company summarized the sentiments of many people when she said, "*I think a lot of project managers I've worked with don't understand the art of avoiding conflict in the first place. Not everything has to be brought to a head.*"

Brenda, an Alpha in the beverage industry, stated similar feelings when she said, "*Conflict is necessary sometimes, but it is not nearly as necessary as we have been led to believe. Usually when I take the time to understand the other person's goals, and try to look at the reasons this person is acting the way they are, I find that I can work out a solution or a compromise that gets everyone what they want.*"

Dan, an information technology Alpha project manager, also expressed wariness when it comes to conflict. "*I've been taught my whole career that conflict is something good, and while that may be true, I think it's the exception for the project manager and not the rule. It's definitely true that conflict slows my projects down. The more I let the conflict build, the longer it will take to resolve it. I make it a practice to address conflict early and resolve it as quickly as possible, and I try to keep things from boiling over unnecessarily."*

Calvin, another Alpha, said, *"My way of dealing with conflict is to not let it see the light of day. I make every project decision actionable. Every assignment I make has accountability and authority built in. When conflict does come up, I get to it quickly. If conflict is the spark, time is gasoline. I got into an argument with another manager years ago, and over time it took on all of the characteristics of a feud. It became bigger than both of us, and that person won't speak to me to this day. My takeaway from that was to do everything I can to catch conflict early. If I resolve it when it's small, I've just saved myself a lot of trouble down the road."*

This sentiment of quick action was articulated repeatedly during interviews with the Alphas.

Angela, an Alpha who works in the travel industry, said, "*Many project managers I see get into trouble because they ignore conflict. It's called withdrawal, but I think for most people it's really denial. They are hoping it will go away, and that doesn't happen very often. Usually it gets bigger until you have no choice but to deal with it.*"

What The Alphas Know

Relationships are a valuable currency, and that currency often affords project managers the opportunity to cross project lines to get things done.

Conflict is a reality that managers must deal with on most projects, but the supposed benefits of conflict may have been overrated in recent years when it comes to projects and project teams. Conflict resolution is a positive outcome, but conflict itself can be a serious hindrance to project progress.

When conflict does arise, Alphas make it a practice to separate the person from the problem. As one of the Alphas, Victor, put it, "*I haven't met a person in business yet that I couldn't get along with. Not every problem can necessarily be resolved, but I won't let that ruin a good relationship if there is any way I can prevent it."*

Alphas make it a practice to catch conflict early. *"If I don't,"* Sarah stressed, *"it will become so big that it will take over my office and be sitting in my chair waiting for me."*

Finally, Alphas don't get tunnel vision when conflict arises on their project. Jarred, another Alpha, said this: *"I have to remind myself, practically daily, that my relationships are just as important as the project. I have a natural inclination to run over people when it comes to conflict, but I have to work with them long after the product has been delivered."*

While conflict may be a growth industry in general, the top managers work hard to keep it firmly in check on their projects.

Nine

Alignment

Alignment is a powerful component of project success, whether it is the project manager's alignment with senior management, the project's alignment with the organization's strategic goals, or the team's alignment with the project manager and the project itself. Just as the wheels of an automobile can cause serious operating problems if they are misaligned, issues with project alignment must be identified and corrected quickly before more serious issues arise, such as performance issues, quality problems, loss of morale or resources, or even complete project failure. This chapter explores differences in alignment between the Alpha and non-Alpha groups.

For the purposes of The Alpha Study, alignment was defined as "the state that exists when the motivations and energies of the stakeholders are compatible with the project, the organization goals, and the constraints, and they are properly invested to see the project succeed."

Alignment can be a very difficult thing to achieve, since the project manager has to factor in numerous intangible aspects, such as motivation and attitude, not only for the teams and other stakeholders, but for himself. If a stakeholder's personal goals are not in alignment with the project's goals, or if the project's goals are not aligned with the external forces driving the project, then a state of misalignment exists, which can negatively influence almost every aspect of the project.

Five Levels of Project Alignment

There are five primary dimensions of project alignment, and while all of them are important, this chapter is primarily concerned with the ones that may be strongly influenced by a project manager, primarily numbers four and five.

Before delving into the dimensions that are the primary responsibility of the project manager, let's explore one aspect of project alignment that is often overlooked.

Alignment of Project to Strategy

Studies indicate that projects which have strong alignment to the performing organization's strategic goals run a lower risk of cancellation, even if the project experiences serious problems. Strategic alignment provides the project and its team with a life vest that can add much needed buoyancy when things get rough. This may be attributed to a number of factors. For instance, the project may have high-level visibility and additional funding may be more readily available, or since the project is strategic, it may be difficult to cancel due to the negative impact on the organization.

Before proceeding further, it should be noted that
most projects performed by businesses are not
strategic. Many are simply routine; however, most
project managers expressed a strong preference
for managing highly strategic projects due to the
opportunities for career advancement, elevated
visibility, and general prestige accompanying such
projects.

In part one of the survey, one of the questions posed
to project managers was this: "Is your primary project
considered highly strategic to your organization
(i.e. , does it strongly contribute to the performing
organization's core strategic goals)?"

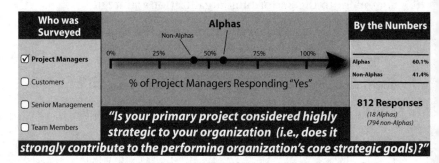

The dramatic difference between the two groups
indicates that there is some awareness of the gap in
strategic alignment; however, self authentication is
rarely a reliable measure, so the same question was

posed to the project managers' senior management.
"Is this project manager's primary project considered
highly strategic to your organization (i.e., does
it strongly contribute to your organization's core
strategic goals)?"

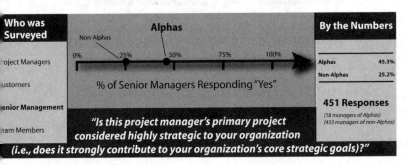

It is worth pointing out that both groups of project
managers estimated that they were managing
strategic projects significantly more often than senior
management, and this gap invited further inquiry. In
follow-up phone interviews of project managers from
both groups, the project managers were asked to name
their organization's top three strategic goals.

Then, senior management evaluated the responses to
determine whether the project manager's answer was
a correct accounting of the organization's top strategic
goals. The results were less than stellar for either
group, revealing another considerable gap between the
Alphas and non-Alphas.

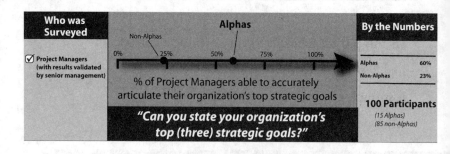

When questioned about this in follow-up interviews, most of the participating project managers felt that they had not received proper downward communication from senior management identifying the organization's top strategic goals.

Gerry, a non-Alpha who took part in the survey, said, "*After participating in this, it really opened my eyes, and I did my own informal poll with the thirty or so project managers in our division at a group meeting. No one knew our strategic goals, and that included my boss and her boss. So after that, I didn't feel so bad about not knowing myself. It has to make its way down from the top.*"

Ken, another non-Alpha, stated another common sentiment. "*I honestly don't know whether my project is strategic or not because it's not my job to focus on strategy. My job is to manage projects, and my third line manager does the strategy. He stays out of my project, and I try to stay out of his business."*

While it is true that most project managers are not actively involved in determining organizational strategy, that does not mean that project managers should be wholly unaware of the organization's strategic goals. If project managers, whether Alpha or non-Alpha, do not know their organization's strategic goals, then it is highly unlikely that they will be able to articulate to the stakeholders whether or how their project contributes to the achievement of those goals.

The attitude of the Alphas on this point may seem similar in many ways to the non-Alphas, but there are substantial differences in the way that the issue of strategic alignment is perceived. One of the Alphas, Cheryl, showed her understanding of this when she said, *"Our top strategic goal for this year has been the launch of five new products in an emerging automobile audio technology. My project really supports all of them indirectly, but the goal is so important that my project is considered highly strategic by [the organization]."*

Understanding how a project aligns to the strategic goals may not make an immediate contribution to the project itself, but it can have a critical impact if the industry, the organization, or the project is in trouble.

Jarred, another Alpha at a transportation and logistics company, took this concept of strategic alignment one step further. *"To me, what is even more important than knowing the organization's strategic goals is to find out how my boss is measured in his annual review. If he gets measured on ROI (return on investment), then I try to make sure my projects reflect ROI. Whatever is important to him is important to me. Maybe it's just a vocabulary issue, but I try to make sure I'm always in line with what is important to him."*

The Project Management Office

One of the questions that this study investigated was whether a Project Management Office (PMO) made any difference as to whether a project manager was a member of the Alpha group. While the Alpha group was not large enough to make sweeping statistical generalizations about the value of a PMO, it did offer some clues.

In part one of the survey, participants were asked whether their organization had a PMO.

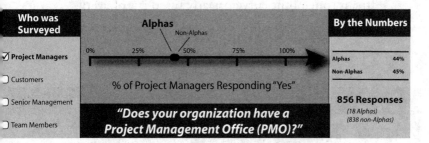

The two groups were virtually identical in their response. Forty-four percent of all organizations represented by the survey had a PMO. When the Alpha group was identified and interviewed post-survey, only two of the 18 Alphas felt that the existence of a PMO had any measurable impact on their ability to manage a project successfully. Most project managers acknowledged the need for a PMO at an organizational level, but the majority did not see the value on an individual project level.

Lori, an Alpha who manages strategic outsourcing projects, said, "*Our PMO works best when it supports the project and not when the project has to support the PMO. There are times when the reporting requirements become a huge drain that doesn't contribute to the customer or the project in any real way.*"

Methodology

In part one of the survey, nearly three out of every four participants indicated that their organization had a formal project methodology.

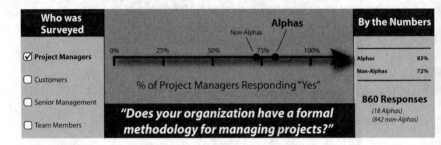

Most project managers provided highly favorable responses when surveyed about the value of their organization's methodology, so part two of the survey focused on the amount of training project managers had received in their organization's methodology.

Project management methodologies are the specific steps, templates, policies, procedures, and practices used to perform a project. Ideally, companies will tailor their methodologies to their business practices and organizational strengths, and that underscores the importance of training. Since most organizations have methodologies that are highly adapted to their business, training becomes paramount.

Part two of the survey asked those who were in
an organization that had a formal methodology:
"How much formal training have you received in
your organization's methodology over the past three
years?" Software-tool training only qualified if the
software was specifically configured to support the
methodology.

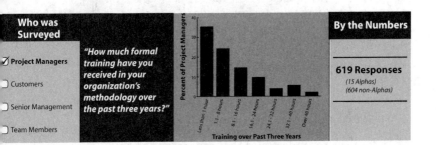

For the entire subset of managers who worked in an
organization that had a formal methodology, more
than one out of every three received less than one
hour of methodology training over the past three
years.

Given the agreed-upon importance of methodologies
and the amount of time and money organizations
invest in them, the number of trained managers
seemed low.

Mike, a non-Alpha project manager, expressed his frustration at the situation. "*We are directed to manage projects in accordance with our methodology. We even sign this piece of paper stating that we will, but I have worked here almost four and a half years now, and no one has ever trained me or any of the managers in our division in our methodology. Everyone uses the templates and examples we are given, but that is about as far as it goes. You figure out that as long as the customer is happy, no one asks you any questions.*"

Based purely on the numbers, most organizations appear to understand the importance of having a methodology but are not entirely sure how to realize the value once it is in place. Along this line, senior management was asked to quantify the value of project management within their organization. It should be no surprise that managers of the Alphas placed a higher value on project management than the managers of the non-Alpha group. This was, in part, due to the fact that in order to qualify as an Alpha, you needed to receive a higher ranking by senior management as well as others.

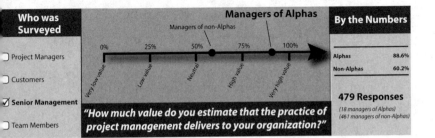

Post survey interviews with senior managers revealed that the value that the managers of Alphas put on project management is, in part, influenced by the way the Alpha group demonstrates value.

Team Alignment

There is a significant body of research on the importance of team alignment, both to the project and the project manager. Traditionally, analysis of this alignment has focused on team performance, seeking to understand whether or not the team was aligned to the project manager and whether their goals and overall motivation were in step with those of the project.

In part two of the survey, over 1,500 team members of survey participants responded to a question that asked about their personal motivation to see the project succeed. The question was intentionally worded to place more emphasis on the team member's personal alignment to the project as opposed to their professional duty. In this case, the responses of both groups were very favorable.

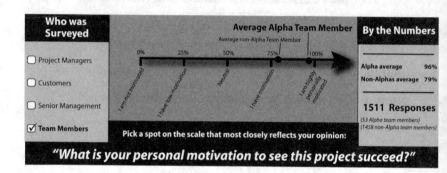

Although both groups had similar results at first glance, post-survey interviews with samples from each group uncovered interesting differences. Over 75% of the team members working on Alpha-managed projects had a feedback loop in place, where the Alpha project manager would provide formal input on their performance appraisal. Additionally, 41% of these same team members had some type of bonus incentive in place tied to their performance.

For team members working on non-Alpha-managed projects, however, only 51% had a feedback loop in place. In other words, half of the project team members had no input given to their functional manager or direct supervisor related to their project performance. For this same group, only 27% had any type of bonus incentive tied to project performance.

Calvin, an Alpha project manager who routinely manages projects with a total project budget of one million dollars and higher, said, "*I always build some bonus money into my project, and I've learned that it doesn't have to be a large sum. The ability to hand out a hundred-dollar reward or even a coupon for a dinner out can make all the difference in someone's attitude. I try to make a big deal about it when I do this so it gets noticed. I try to work it so that the reward reflects the achievement, but anything is better than just ignoring something that deserves recognition.*"

What The Alphas Know

As discussed in Chapter Two, the team and senior management had substantial influence on which project managers were Alphas and which were not. As many project managers pointed out, it can be very challenging to manage the expectations of both groups, as they often have conflicting goals;

yet this task speaks to the heart of what makes
the Alpha group stand out from the other 98%.
They understand how to manage down without
compromising the need to deliver results to senior
management, and they are able to manage up without
alienating the team.

Alphas know the importance of aligning the project to
the goals of the organization, and just as importantly,
they communicate not only regarding the project
goals, but also regarding the organizational goals.

Alphas also know the importance of ensuring that
the team is strongly aligned to the project. While
many team members will work hard for the project
out of professional responsibility, individuals require
strong personal motivation before optimal team
performance can be achieved. There are many forms
that this motivation can take, including recognition,
praise, and financial incentive. Although both groups
acknowledge this, the Alphas formally build it into
the projects far more often.

Finally, the Alpha project managers work to convince their senior managers of the value of project management. As one of the Alphas, Angela, summed it up, *"My manager is fanatical about project management, and that makes my job so much easier in almost every way imaginable!"*

Ten α

Issue Management

While project management flourished beginning in the late twentieth and early twenty-first centuries, one of the areas that has been largely overlooked is that of issue management. Only recently has issue management garnered any real prominence in project management; however, it still does not have equal standing with such core topics as scope, quality, or schedule management.

Unlike the rest of this book, the information in this chapter did not come primarily from the surveys. Instead, it was derived primarily from post-survey interviews with project managers and stakeholders. It is less numerical and statistical than the topics discussed in the other chapters.

When surveyed and interviewed on the subject of issue management, project managers were not always responsive; however, when post-interview surveys were conducted, senior management and customers spoke freely.

One of the challenges of issue management is that issues may touch on virtually any area of a project and may arise at any time. One project manager likened issue management to fighting the mythical hydra. When one head was cut off, two more replaced it. Likewise, the more he tried to shorten his list of issues, the longer the list grew.

Over a dozen working variations on the definition of an issue already exist within project management, and each one carries its own subtleties and priorities. For the purpose of this survey, an issue was defined as *"an important project-related question, the answer to which is unknown, is in dispute, or which threatens the project."*

The number of issues over the life of a project has a strong correlation to the number of active stakeholders; however, that is not a sufficient model to predict issues. Technical complexity, mission criticality, size of scope, length of schedule, numbers of users, and funding sources are just a few of the factors that can contribute to the list and intensity of issues on a project.

Post-survey interviews with project managers, senior management, and customers identified significant differences between the Alpha and non-Alpha groups in the way issues were identified, handled, and resolved. In particular, the Alphas and their managers provided insights into the methods they employed to manage issues to overall stakeholder satisfaction.

Ability to Negotiate

One of the most prominent techniques that the Alpha group exhibited was the ability to negotiate with stakeholders over issues. While this negotiation took on several forms, it almost always resulted in a shorter issue list.

One of the Alphas, Lori, uses time as a negotiating tool to keep the issue list under control. "*In my business, a lot of issues are brought up in the heat of the moment and can suddenly take on a life of their own.*

I put a waiting period in place before something can become an issue. Even if it's just two or three days, I like to have a short period of time where everyone gets a chance to consider things and calm down. Then if it's still an issue, we can put it on the log and take the appropriate steps. Of course, some issues are obvious and serious and I have the ability to bypass the waiting list, but most are not. This keeps a lot of issues from ever seeing the light of day."

Sarah, an Alpha in the telecommunications industry, said, *"Some issues are objective, and they'll stop the project whether you acknowledge them or not, but most of the issues on my projects are really very subjective. They represent opinions, and sometimes it's as easy as a conversation with one person to get that issue removed from the list."*

Instead of dutifully documenting and logging everything brought up as an issue, most of the Alphas expressed variations on the above strategies to keep issues from ever going on the list.

Brenda, a project manager in the soft drink industry, stated her strategy this way: *"A lot of things that get managed as issues simply aren't issues at all. An issue is not a difference of opinion or a disagreement. An issue is something that threatens my project. That could be a threat against the scope, against the schedule, or against the budget, but that's about it. Most anything else doesn't get put on the issue log on my projects. I used to write down every single question or concern and treat it like an issue, but if you treat something like an issue, it will become an issue, and then you'll really have something to deal with. You don't ever want the issue log itself to become another issue."*

The concept that most issues on a project may not be issues at all is striking when one considers the amount of time and resources that are invested into resolving them. Customers interviewed repeatedly stated that they had fewer project issues with those who made the Alpha list. In reality, it was just as likely that there was as great a difference in what was actually managed as an issue as how it was managed.

Issue Management Techniques

Just like the other factors which impact the ultimate success of the project, issues must be aggressively managed. While many in the non-Alpha group did not have a formal set of procedures in place for managing issues, the Alphas almost always kept the appropriate focus and prioritization on the issue log.

Jim, an Alpha in construction, keeps the issue log in front of him throughout the project. "*I always keep hardcopy of four things on my desk: the critical success factors for the project, the schedule, some financial reports, and the issue log, and I've found that the later it gets in the project, the less important the first three become, and the more important the issue log becomes. Any issue that touches one of the critical success factors gets a special priority and gets addressed right away.*"

Another Alpha, Kyle, works in the information technology outsourcing industry, where a single issue may have legal implications and account for very large sums of money. "*The one thing you can count on in any significant project is that there will be issues, and issue management is one of those things that I am very careful about. I keep my issues ranked by urgency, and I can tell you the top four or five off the top of my head at any point in time. These get the lion's share of my management attention.*"

The philosophy that issue management gets special attention was much more prevalent among the Alphas than the non-Alphas. When discussing their overall approach to project management, the Alphas regularly mentioned issue management as an integral part, while the non-Alpha group was more likely to stick to topics that have historically received more attention.

The type and frequency of issues on the project can give a strong indication of the overall project health. Thomas, an Alpha in commercial software, said, "*I use the number of critical issues as a kind of thermometer for my project. One project I managed was completely overrun by issues, and managing them became a full time job for me, but it was indicative of something else that was occurring on the project. What was actually going on was that the whole reason for doing the project had changed. The market had shifted, and the reasons that were driving us when we started were no longer present. The number of critical issues that were starting to filter in was a good indicator that there were real problems going on.*"

Melinda, an Alpha in biotechnology, said, "*Issues are important, but they almost always translate into delays.*

The rule on my projects is 'keep working.' People like to call a lot of issues 'showstoppers' that really shouldn't even slow a project down, much less bring things to a halt. The one thing I've learned over the last twenty years or so is that progress on a project resolves most issues by itself."

Escalation

Knowing when to bring an issue to senior management or the customer can be a difficult task, and it will likely differ project to project and customer to customer. Escalating issues inappropriately communicates incompetence or a lack of confidence, while not escalating enough signals that the project manager is secretive or not willing to communicate. There is a small space in between where project managers communicate openly and effectively with their stakeholders.

A fine line exists between communication and escalation, and discussions with project managers revealed that most of them struggle with finding this line.

Assessment

Gerald, a senior manager of Victor, one of the Alphas, had this to say about his issue management. "*Victor has a great knack for getting to the heart of an issue. He can take a problem, decide whether or not it is an issue, and know exactly what to do with it. And he does this very quickly. I have worked with project managers who blow issues out of proportion or just freeze when an issue comes up, but Victor has this ability to size up a situation very accurately and take the necessary steps to deal with it.*"

Marty, an Alpha in the defense industry, said, "*Like it or not, I put a section in my report of the most serious potential issues facing me on the project. That is just for communication's sake. If it's really important, I'll bring it up in a meeting with the customer or my boss, but if it's something I have under control, I don't like to raise concerns.*"

Many project managers seem to think that the image that everything is under control is paramount, whether or not it is true. Repeatedly in follow-up interviews, project managers stated that they felt it

was their job to shield stakeholders from the issues. As
Deborah, a non-Alpha, stated, *"It's my job to manage
issues. If other people start becoming aware of issues
on my project, then I'm not doing my job. The more I
involve people in the nuts and bolts of my job, the less
value I am providing."*

But in a separate interview, Deborah's manager stated
a different sentiment. *"It seems to be that the more
serious the issue is, the less likely I am to find out about it
right away. Project managers want to communicate that
things are all under control, but I was a PM for years, so
I know that this is rarely the case. I'd rather be presented
with the facts and make up my own mind as to whether
or not I should be concerned."*

Resolution

Carl, a senior manager responsible for a division of
over a dozen project managers, said, *"No matter how
good you are at planning, you will have issues at some
point in the project. The easiest way for me to tell a
seasoned PM from someone just starting out is to see how
quickly they can drive issues to completion. The more
mature a project manager is, the more they will get very*

'hawkish' on important issues and close them out as soon as possible. Beginners seem to hope most of them will just go away."

Dave, an Alpha in the insurance industry, said this: "*It helps me to think of issues as having real weight, just like a rock. When issues multiply on one of my projects, I visualize rocks being dumped into my backpack. I can keep going, only much more slowly than before. If I'm carrying around a backpack full of rocks, then everything I do is affected. To put it in real terms, if I am on a project with few issues, and I need to make a technical product decision, I can usually do that quickly and easily. But if I have several project issues, then that means that I'm probably going to have to run my decision by more people and go through processes I wouldn't otherwise. That translates to slowing me down just like rocks in my backpack. The net of it is that I try not to let them accumulate. I'm consistently moving issues off my issue list.*"

Another Alpha, Sarah, commented on the potentially negative power of issues. "*About eight years ago, I had a large project that was going along just fine until it was unexpectedly cancelled. The company cut their budget, and one project had to go, and it was mine. The deciding factor came down to the fact that I had too many open issues on my issue log. The reality was that the project was going just fine, but I did have a lot of issues on the log. Since then, I've taken that lesson to heart. When an issue goes onto the log, I work very hard to close it out as soon as possible, and a lot of things that people think are issues never make it to the log because they don't belong there."*

Another senior manager in the automotive industry, who also serves as a project customer, said, *"Most of the PMs in my organization don't seem to know why their [issue log] is even there. It's a tool for organizing, prioritizing, communicating, and closing issues. I wish more of them managed the issue log with the same care they managed the initial scope."*

What The Alphas Know

Alphas are very careful with issue management, starting with issue definition. Those in the Alpha group may spend almost as much time trying to keep something from becoming an issue as they would to manage the issue itself. A large number of issues becomes an issue of its own.

Another area where the Alpha group distinguishes itself is in the way issues are escalated to senior management and the customer. The Alphas are able to manage the flow of information in a way that meets the needs of their stakeholders, which implies that their efforts are tailored to meet the stakeholders' expectations.

Managing issues also requires that stakeholders are interests are understood and balanced. By managing this process carefully and transparently, Alphas improve the overall health of their projects.

Eleven α

Leadership

Leadership presents the ultimate bottleneck for business. Organizations, departments, and projects rarely rise past the level of their leadership, and nearly every business problem can inevitably be traced back to a leadership problem. If this is true at the organizational level, it certainly holds true at the individual project level.

As a topic, however, project leadership remains largely overlooked, even with the frenzy of attention that has fallen on general project management. This lack of focus on the topic of leadership has caused many people to confuse leadership and management, blurring the lines between the two. While it helps a good leader if they are also a strong manager, it is not always essential; however, a great manager needs good leadership skills, especially when responsibilities include managing people.

Leading vs. Managing

The nature of project management is such that ad-hoc teams are assembled, with a project manager often assigned who has little positional authority over them. Functional or line managers may lead with both positional authority and the legitimate authority of having a team that reports to them. Project managers often have to make do with neither, regularly being asked to lead a project without a formal commission and with no permanent staff reporting to them. Those who are not strong leaders will struggle in this environment, with each team member motivated by personal factors and not necessarily aligned to project goals.

While the traditional focus of project management has been on an individual's general management skills, knowledge of process, or domain expertise, the qualities of leadership the manager possesses are just as likely to make or break the project.

Good managers deliver results, while good leaders develop people, and in most organizations, successful project managers need to be able to do both. This makes the topic of leadership all the more critical to project managers struggling to lead teams and to deliver results.

On projects where team members, scopes, schedules, budgets, and environments are similar, leadership can easily make the difference between project success and failure. This ingredient is nearly essential to project success. Only a very few projects succeed in spite of their leaders; most succeed because of them.

General business is well aware of the value of strong leadership, and there is good reason for this. Solid leadership transcends market problems, team issues, supplier problems, organizational dysfunction, and almost anything your project will throw at you. Strong leaders can motivate teams to do what they could not as individuals.

There are innumerable examples of how a cohesive team performs better than a group of individuals, such as the Battle of Watling Street, or the men's

hockey championship in the 1980 Olympics. Strong
leadership is what forges a strong team, and while
it would be out of the scope of this chapter to take
on a general discussion of project leadership, it does
explore the common elements of leadership displayed
by the Alpha group.

To begin with, senior managers were polled on their
views on the topic. The group was asked to report the
percentage of projects that failed, in their opinion,
due to a lack of leadership. The results were striking.

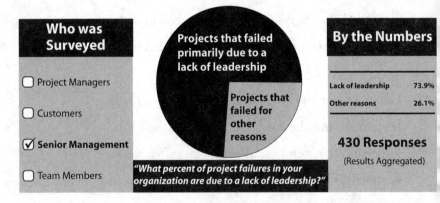

One of the senior managers, Carl, observed, "*Our
company started putting project managers through
leadership simulation training about two years ago, and
that has made a really big difference. The more I look
at it, the more convinced I become that leadership is the
make-or-break skill in project management.*"

This line of questioning was expanded to include customers, senior managers, and team members. Rather than ask the project managers to rank their own effectiveness, the survey asked the question of the stakeholders.

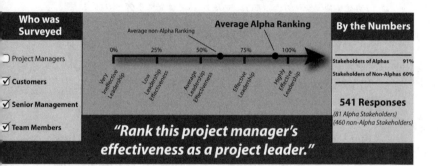

Interestingly, many responses were not counted, since the stakeholders were not always clear on the difference between leadership and management. Out of the 541 responses, however, a gap of 31 percentage points emerged.

In a follow-up interview, one customer of a non-Alpha offered her views on the subject. *"We had a recent high-profile failure that was picked apart by some of the trade journals, and their conclusion was that there was no apparent reason why the project failed. It had everything going for it, and no one could understand why it fell apart, but I believe the reason is very clear: the guy running the project had no concept of how to lead his team, and the team turnover was incredible. It was easy to hire people onto the project because the work and location were very appealing, but after they worked for [the project manager] for a few weeks, they would quit without warning. There was never a sense of team or common purpose on the project."*

Modern leadership theory recognizes that different leadership styles work better in different situations. Fielder's Contingency Model, in particular, shows how the very attributes that make leaders successful in one environment may work against them in a different environment. Successful managers will often tailor their style from project to project, and even over the lifetime of a single project. A manager may begin the project in a very strong, directing style of leadership and soften his approach as the project progresses, changing to a more supporting style as the team forms its identity.

Leadership can be a difficult thing to measure on a survey. Leadership includes a broad set of characteristics, and people will sometimes confuse it with a strong personality or other attributes. For purposes of clarity on the topic, structured interviews were employed with stakeholders of the Alphas and a representative sample of stakeholders of the non-Alphas to discuss how leadership impacted the project team, deliverables, and constraints.

Mike, a team member assigned to a non-Alpha project manager, had this to say: "*I think my project manager would qualify as an 'average leader' if that isn't an oxymoron. He does a good job of leading the team, but he doesn't show leadership with the customer, so the team is constantly getting tossed around by whatever is the customer's hot-button issue this week. I actually think that the complete opposite would be better.*"

Karey, a team member of Jarred, an Alpha in the transportation and logistics industry, commented on the positive aspects of strong leadership. "*I am lucky enough to work for a very strong project leader. I've had it both ways in the past, and when the project manager steps up and leads, it makes all the difference. When there is no strong leadership, then it leaves a vacuum, and things can get very ugly. I have worked on projects that have gotten completely derailed because different people were all trying to step in and fill that vacuum simultaneously.*"

Indeed, several team members commented independently about the tendency of some managers to try to improve the cohesiveness of their teams by befriending them.

Melinda, an Alpha in biotechnology, said, "*For years I tried to befriend team members and gain their loyalty that way, but then a manager told me one time that teams don't need a friend – they need a leader. I wasn't able to hear that at the time, but it did eventually sink in, and now I get what he meant. Teams want someone they can trust and respect. If they also like me, then that is fine, but these days I really try to be the kind of project manager people want to work for.*"

Another Alpha, Sudhir, believes that leadership is crucial in how the work is delegated. "*I am very fair and very careful in how I assign the work. It's important to me that everyone is very clear on what is expected and that they feel empowered to get it done. I don't want someone running into my office several times a day to ask my permission about doing their job. But this is the kind of thing you have to demonstrate and model for the team. You can't just expect everyone to start behaving that way. It takes time. That's why I work really hard to protect my team once they really start to work as a team.*"

Marty, an Alpha in the defense industry, said this about leading the team: "*One thing that can destroy a team is complaining. There is an art to complaining. One simple thing I learned in the military was to complain up but never complain down to my team. I make sure that if I'm complaining to my boss or my customer that I'm very specific about what I want the outcome to be. Pure griping is a waste for everyone involved.*"

Victor, an Alpha in business process consulting, said, "*I don't know of any shortcuts when it comes to leadership. It isn't about what you say; it's all about what you do. It's a tricky thing to balance, because I've seen project managers try to show leadership by sticking up for their team all the time, and the team really likes them, but they may neglect the customer or the company, and that doesn't work. Leadership means balance as much as anything. It means doing the right thing for the team, for the customer, for the company, and for the project. When those things aren't aligned, something has to give, and that's where leadership becomes really important. Asking your team to work overtime because it's the right thing to do takes leadership, but sometimes standing up to the customer and refusing to shift the burden onto your team can take even more leadership.*"

What the Alphas Know

When it came to the subject of leadership, the Alphas received much higher marks from their stakeholders than their counterparts; yet, during interviews, most project managers, even the Alphas, had difficulty summarizing their approach. Both groups regularly commented on the importance of *"doing the right thing"* and how that contributed to their success; however, many stakeholders were not impressed with the efforts of their project managers.

In general, Alphas made a strong distinction between leading and managing. Many of the project managers exhibited strong management abilities, but strong leadership was unusual. The Alphas viewed leadership as an integral topic, touching every activity rather than something that only came up from time to time. It wove its way into everything from project assignment, to delegation of work, to product acceptance.

The Alphas also displayed an understanding that being a strong leader did not necessarily equate with popularity. Being liked on the project was secondary to being respected, which serves as a counterbalance to the discussion on relationships in Chapter Eight.

The high marks that the Alphas received in this area show that they not only were able to lead teams, but they also were able to demonstrate leadership to senior management and the customer. With the Alpha group, it was visible to parties in all directions.

Twelve

What the Alphas Know

In the physical world, even things that appear identical will reveal variances when measured with enough precision. We live in a universe that is full of variation, and that variation makes things interesting.

No matter how much standardization takes place in the world of project management, no matter how uniform the processes, or how consistent the templates or procedures, there will always be a top 2%, and only a sliver of the overall population will lay claim to that ranking. Not everyone can achieve the top 2%, but most people can achieve a measure of excellence in their work. In reality, the traits that separate the top 2% from the top 33% often turn out to be so small and subtle as to seem insignificant at first glance. But insignificant they are not. Football, it has been said, is a game of inches. Project management can be viewed the same way. What separates the successful projects from the failures may seem arcane or difficult for the novice or the unobservant to detect. What separates the top project managers from everyone else is likely much less than most people think.

It is easy to get lost in the details of a project such as The Alpha Study, focusing on statistical significance, confidence intervals, and correlation, so it is important to examine the bigger picture. The Alpha Study took a careful look at the practices and attitudes of 860 project managers and cross-referenced numerous attributes against thousands of stakeholders. The data from this study were analyzed for statistically significant findings, and follow-up interviews were conducted to try and understand why trends and gaps existed where they did.

The purpose of The Alpha Study was to understand what the top performers do that sets them apart. It sought to answer questions about what one group knew that the others did not, the impact of hard work, how attitude contributed to overall success, and what were the basic beliefs, habits, and practices within project management that led to the success of the Alpha group.

Many of the people who were exposed to The Alpha Study asked questions that ultimately came down to this: "*What can I do to be an Alpha?*" That simple question has sparked debate over the definition of success in career, the contribution of work environment, and nature vs. nurture.

The immutable reality is, no matter how much progress is made in theory or practice within project management, 98% of the population will not be in the top 2% at any given point in time. Rather than ask what one can do to become an Alpha, a better approach is to ask what we can learn from the Alphas in order to improve our performance. Fortunately, there is "low-hanging fruit" that the great majority of project managers can implement to see a significant improvement in their performance.

Environment

As discussed in Chapter Nine, there was a dramatic difference in the attitudes of the Alphas' senior managers and the senior managers of the other 98%. Almost without exception, Alpha project managers work in organizations that support project management. This means that these organizations typically have a defined career path for project managers, and while they may not always have a project management office, they do have well-defined methodologies. This is in sharp contrast to the organizations where many project managers are viewed as overhead or are considered a necessary evil.

Environmental factors certainly affect the success of project managers. It is highly likely that if the Alphas were put into environments where project management was not valued, they would not have excelled to the degree they did. It would be a misconception, however, to assume that being an Alpha is all about what organization you work for. It is most definitely not. To use a metaphor, if an Alpha is a race car, then the organization may be thought of as a well-maintained track. Both are necessary for high performance, but the organization by itself cannot produce Alphas. In fact, it is telling that no two Alphas were from the same organization, and most were from altogether different industries.

For project managers who work in an organization where their discipline is not appreciated, it may be nearly impossible to become an Alpha. The reason for this is simple: being an Alpha is not a one-person job. It requires the support and cooperation of whole teams of people working in concert. If an organization is resistant to project management, then the necessary level of cooperation is unlikely to exist. While environment may be largely out of a project manager's control, there are likely steps that can be taken to improve the environment in which a project manager works.

One way to improve the work environment is to heighten awareness of the value of project management as a discipline. In many companies, the benefits of project management are not highly visible. Ironically, this can be most true when the project is running smoothly. It is human nature to take such things for granted. With no crisis and no problems, some senior managers and organizations may wrongly assume that the project would run just as smoothly with no management at all. This underscores the importance of making project management visible.

One important way the Alphas influence their environments is by measuring and reporting meaningful metrics, particularly the metrics of time, money, and customer satisfaction. There was a keen awareness of the value of project management among the senior managers of the Alpha group, but this was largely due to the fact that the Alphas worked throughout the project life cycle to make them aware. When a project manager does his or her job well and reports on accurate financial and schedule data, the question of whether or not project management is necessary falls by the wayside.

Commitment to Improvement

One of the interesting things about the Alpha group is that they were far more likely to discuss what they did not do well than they were to brag about their accomplishments. This characteristic points to a high-degree of self-awareness and a desire to improve. There was a degree of genuine humility present in this group that was not evident in the overall population.

Everyone has professional blind spots. There is a wide variance in our ability to accurately gauge how we are perceived in the workplace, and it is likely that no one has a completely accurate view of his strengths, weaknesses, or how others perceive them. The recent rise in popularity of 360° reviews may be one component of the answer. By facilitating reviews from parties who interact with the manager in several different ways, project managers get input from all directions that helps them gauge their overall performance. Benefiting from the real results of a 360° review, however, requires that individual to have a degree of emotional maturity, as well as the confidence to receive and properly apply criticism. When a high degree of honesty is encouraged, this tool can be particularly beneficial for the project manager. By providing a safe and, in some cases, anonymous environment for people to give feedback on the manager's performance from varying perspectives, project managers can gain valuable (if sometimes painful) insight into how others perceive them.

Most project managers were largely unaware of how their teams, customers, and senior managers actually perceived their performance. They were highly focused on the product they were delivering but were mostly unaware of how they were doing their job. Without an accurate assessment, managers may assume the wrong thing.

As The Alpha Study revealed time and again, many of the non-Alphas, and particularly those in the bottom third of the composite index, viewed their contributions, skills, and abilities very differently than did their managers, team members, and customers. The most common scenario was for managers to view their personal communication or leadership effectiveness as very high, while most stakeholders took a less favorable view. This was occasionally true for the Alpha group as well, but it was consistently true for non-Alphas.

If managers do not have an accurate view of how they are perceived in their jobs, they will not be able to take the steps to correct weak areas. Many managers have been frustrated to find that the areas that are most important to them have a very low ranking with the stakeholders.

Relationships

A universal theme among the Alphas is that they have solid relational skills. This is not to say that being an Alpha was a popularity contest. There were several objective measures in place to ensure that the Alphas consistently delivered on the scope, time, and cost objectives of the project, but many revealed in post-survey interviews that their success at managing projects was proportional to the strength of their relationships.

Managing relationships is a difficult task for many people to learn, but it would be extremely difficult to rise to the top of this field (or any other for that matter) without strong relational skills.

Human beings, by and large, have blind spots, and project managers are certainly no exception. Most project managers believe they are doing their jobs very well, while most stakeholders are less enthralled with the project manager's performance. The reason is that all too often they have separate goals and separate criteria for judging success.

Whereas the project manager's main responsibility is to deliver the product, service, or result on time and within budget, how he carries out this duty will influence his success. A project manager that alienates stakeholders, keeps team members in the dark, and holds senior management at arm's length can only expect problems.

Communication

Project managers who participated in the Alpha Study were asked to share their strongest lesson learned from the end of their most recent project. The overwhelming share of the popular vote went to the area of "communication." Among practically everyone who touches a project, there is a general awareness that communication could be better; everyone, that is, except for the project manager who is ultimately responsible for communicating. To this point, a staggering 91% of project managers ranked their effective communication higher than their collective stakeholders did. It seems those sending the communication have very different criteria than those receiving it.

Without exception, the 18 Alphas proved to be outstanding communicators. Their skills came across in written correspondence, interviews, and general discussions. Although they were not the only good communicators, this skill was consistently present in the project managers ranked in the top tiers.

Good communication is comprised of more than how the message is delivered. The information itself, the method used, and the timing with which it is delivered all contribute to effective communication. Few topics evoked the emotional responses of the stakeholders that communication did. Numerous senior managers, customers, and team members indicated that this was their single greatest need. Complaints were consistently directed at the quality, quantity, and frequency of the communication they received.

While good communication alone does not make a great project manager, it is arguably impossible to be a great project manager without being at least a good communicator. Communication is the lifeblood of the project. It is the way that stakeholders feel connected and empowered. As Victor stated, "*Until my product is in the customer's hands, communication is my deliverable."*

It is hard to overstate the emphasis top project managers put on communication, but the attitude runs deeper than simply an emphasis. The higher a project manager's ranking by stakeholders, the more likely he was to believe that communication was generally an asset. Indeed, the Alpha project managers overwhelmingly expressed their belief in their ability to use communication to help the project, while the non-Alphas, and particularly those at the lower end of the scale, more often expressed concern that their communication was often used against them.

These views seem to become self-fulfilling prophecies. The Alpha group communicates frequently, predictably, and accurately. The non-Alphas hoard information, especially bad information, and they keep their stakeholders in the dark as long as possible, expressing surprise when stakeholder frustrations erupt.

Just like compounding interest can work for or against you, depending on which side of the equation you are on, communication can be a strong project asset, or it can work to undermine and ultimately destroy a project.

Mentoring

Whether it is diagnosing our own illness or evaluating the way in which we relate to coworkers and employees, human beings are traditionally not strong at assessing their own strengths and weaknesses. It is nearly impossible for us to see ourselves the way others see us. Committing to self-improvement is one of the most difficult things to do. People are largely creatures of habit, falling into familiar patterns of behavior.

This is good news for those wishing to rise to the top of the field, for it means that success will probably not require radical change in performance or a doubling of effort. Rather, improvement is perhaps a process of fine tuning and incremental change that begins with a willingness to evaluate everything dispassionately. Mentoring relationships can be a tremendous help in this regard, but it is not only the act of being mentored that can make a difference here. The act of mentoring may have a positive influence on both parties.

Angela formally mentors two project managers outside of her industry. *"We meet twice a month for breakfast, and I find that it really allows me time to stop thinking about the way things are and to think about how things should be. Sometimes when we meet and we're discussing a situation at work or on a project, I can see what the other person should be doing, but I have to ask myself, 'Do I follow my own advice in this area?'"*

Mentoring can provide time for both project managers to analyze and discuss processes, approaches, and specific situations outside of the working environment. It allows everyone to step back and reflect on the bigger picture, and it provides a time to solicit specific advice.

Another Alpha, Dan, commented on the benefits he has experienced in mentoring relationships. *"I have had two different mentors over the past three years, one of them internal to my company, and one external. To me, the biggest benefit is just taking the time to discuss project management with someone else. That one-on-one interaction pays benefits you just can't get from reading a book or sitting through a class."*

Whether mentoring or being mentored, the time spent brings valuable, focused perspective. Additionally, mentoring can help expand the project manager's network.

Leadership

If strong communication can be a "quick win" for many project managers, leadership is typically a longer process. Leading people is not easy, nor are the necessary skills developed quickly.

Many project managers demonstrated the basic skills to be an Alpha but failed the "leadership test" in the eyes of their stakeholders. They could do all of the basic management duties expected of a project manager, but they could not lead teams. This one component kept a large number out of the running for Alpha consideration.

Holding all other skills at a baseline, leadership is a differentiating factor, yet most project managers expressed difficulty and confusion with the topic. Many could not tell the difference between the topics of leadership and management, and few understood the importance of tailoring their leadership style to a particular situation.

One problem is that universities are preparing management graduates to organize and manage tasks, but few of these individuals are being graduated with the skills or experience needed to lead teams. This places a "choke point" on the project, constraining performance, and teams rarely outperform their leaders.

Many teams are indifferent or ambivalent toward the project manager (at best). They do not look at the project manager as a leader because the project manager does not lead.

Conclusion

The Alpha Study investigated several dimensions of a project manager's belief and practice to understand the difference between the top performers and the rest. It explored the broad topics of attitude and belief, focus and prioritization, communication, approach, relationships and conflict, alignment, issue management, and leadership.

Within these topics, it is almost universally true that small things can make a big difference. The gap between the Alphas and the other 98% of the population may be quite large on some levels; however, most of this is caused by very subtle behaviors and differences. Both groups show up for work, plan their projects, manage their teams, deliver the results, and gain the customer's acceptance. In most regards, what they have in common is much greater than what separates them. Professional sprinters often finish within hundredths of a second of each other, yet the ones who win do so consistently.

When an entire population possesses highly similar characteristics, any advantage, however small, can have very significant implications. Small differences in behavior and practices can account for large outcomes, both actual and perceived. That is, perhaps, the single most powerful truth that the Alphas know that everyone else does not.

Project managers need not aspire to become Alphas in order to challenge themselves to be better at their jobs. Self improvement should be treated as a process instead of a project, and this process rarely provides instant gratification. While the majority of the qualities demonstrated by the Alpha group are squarely within the reach of most project managers, the process of developing them requires time and a deep, ongoing commitment to continuous personal and professional growth.

Project managers who undertake this challenge will almost certainly find that the rewards extend far beyond their careers.

Index